TOURN

ENTER
YOUR
INITIALS
for record keeping

COBALT PRESS
Baltimore, MD

Enter Your Initials for Record Keeping

Copyright © 2015
ISBN: 978-1-941462-13-3
Cover design by Amanda Gilleland
Book design by Andrew Keating

Cobalt Press
Baltimore, MD

cobaltreview.com/cobalt-press

For all inquiries, including requests for review materials, please contact andrewk@cobaltpress.org.

For Eddie O

ENTER YOUR INITIALS

for record keeping

[BRI]

DALLAS MAVERICKS

The first thing you need to know is that the game is not basketball. It is far too glamorous to be called that; it is an ode to what we imagine ourselves doing if we had the chance; it is a fantasy simulator. It is not strategy; it is not jump shots from the corner, screens being set, boxing out the last defender. It is not chest-passes, Xs and Os, picks and rolls, set shots. Your grandfather does not turn on the television on Sunday afternoons to watch this: you, drinking soda from cans solely so you can go out in the garage and crush the aluminum into discs, so you can fling them into a garbage can. Him, pointing out trajectories—of how hard it must be

1

not to lose the ball in the wake of heads, all wearing the same color, all hands in the air. It is nothing that you've ever seen.

What you do is not basketball either: clumsy and slow, holding the ball near your shoulder and jumping as high as you can. You, using your arms for power instead of your legs, despite what your father told you, despite what everyone has ever told you. It is difficult to understand these things when you are ten—that you could do this all so much easier if you were taller, that you are growing taller—even taller than you are wide, and that the day will come when you do not need to worry about the release point of your shot because you will simply jump up in the air and throw the ball though the hoop, that no one will need to teach you any of that—that you're tall for your age, that you are growing taller.

In the same way that soccer is the beautiful game, in the same way that boxing is the sweet science, these things are not all that they are if they are not handled correctly: no one would ever call a missed kick gorgeous; there are no slow-motion shots of a punch to the eye in a lunch-room brawl.

In the game, you play Dallas first—a team with zero identity and almost as many wins in the early 1990s; all of their players injured or old. The team consists of Derek Harper, the Mavericks' perennial point guard, and Mike Iuzzolino, a player who disappeared from the league almost immediately, a trivia answer, a fun fact. This is not a man you dream about being, but there he is: jumping higher than the moon, making shots from every angle. There is no romance to this—a man who no one picks, a man with no poster.

When we play games, we play the same things over and over again. I cannot tell you the amount of times that I've run through the first few screens of Super Mario Bros, the amount of times

I've knifed the first boss in the bar in Ninja Gaiden. Here, it is similar. There is familiarity here—that all games go through Iuzzolino, that anyone who put their quarters up saw him, forgettable but familiar. The only way you avoid this is to be the Mavericks, to forget that Derek Harper went from the worst team to the best in a trade with the Knicks, to embody Iuzzolino, to be the first turtle shell kicked, to be the office wastepaper champion, to crush every can to create something smaller, yet less hollow. To recognize that the worst this game has to offer is still larger than anything you can grip with your palm.

It depends what your definition of *is* is. It depends what your definition of *him* is. Is he a teammate? An opponent? Is he William Jefferson Clinton? Is he Slick Willie? Is he just *Bill*?

His Secret Service code name was—still is, I assume—*Eagle*, a high flyer, endangered, protected. Hillary's was *Evergreen*, Chelsea's *Energy*. With these names, they moved around in DC and the world, apart from us.

I have never seen a president, although I have had close encounters with some. When I was in high school, Clinton's motorcade passed by at the end of my block, on its way to a TV station. Several black cars drove by me as I watched from behind a

WASHINGTON BULLETS

PLAYER 2

[RAF]

barricade. I never knew which one he was in. It had barely been 30 years since Kennedy died in a motorcade; Kennedy, who shook Clinton's teenaged hand.

My senior year of high school, three friends and I disdained our classmates' trips to South Padre Island and instead drove from Kansas City to Colorado where we stayed with two of my aunts, a few days with each. Most days, we drove around Denver and Boulder, hiking and buying records, eating cheaply and running through the dozen or so tapes in my car's stereo. By mid-week, we were lazy and tired, and we relocated to my Aunt Karen's house, where my cousin owned a Sega Genesis with *NBA Jam*.

We played it incessantly for three days. It was the only time I have ever played the game. I did not know that, if I entered the initials ARK, I could play as Bill Clinton.

Twenty years since those three days. Usually, I don't feel middle-aged, but I suppose that I am. I haven't seen the three guys I played *NBA Jam* with in a very long time. One still lives in Kansas City. One lives in New Jersey. I don't know where the third is.

Now, I live in Virginia, and spend a day or two each month in Washington, DC. Sometimes in the District, I'll pass the Verizon Center, home of the Washington Wizards, formerly the Washington Bullets, a team vanished because its name was too violent. I never see anyone wearing old Bullets gear, although most of the people I see in these sections of DC are tourists, staring at maps as they try to get from Ford's Theater to the Air and Space Museum (go down 10th, take a left on Pennsylvania, then a right on 7th. It's across the Mall).

There's a lot that's gone here. There's a lot that's gone everywhere.

The year I drove across Kansas with my friends, the Bullets traded Tom Gugliotta, the only Bullet to appear on all platforms of *NBA Jam*, to the Golden State Warriors. They got Chris Webber in exchange, and Webber injured his shoulder not long after.

There is that chance to inhabit someone else's life; to do the impossible: *I can leap over a flaming barrel. I can shoot an arrow into the demon's eye. I can kick a snake so hard it vanishes in a puff of smoke.*

I suppose democracy works in the same way that video games do; I vote for a candidate, and if they win, then they represent me, they are my avatar. I am my president, my senators, my representative, my mayor, my delegate, my electors, my city council representative, my department chair, my committee chair. From the Choose a Player One screen I chose them. It sounds naïve. It sounds like high school civics. It sounds like something a Boy Scout would say, but, then again, I was a Boy Scout.

Clinton was younger than I am now when he was first elected governor of Arkansas. There are three players older than me still playing in the NBA. Tom Gugliotta retired in 2005. He was two years younger than I am now. One version of *NBA Jam* spelled his name "Gugliotti." The Bullets changed their name to the Wizards in 1997. You can buy a Bullets jersey pretty inexpensively on eBay. It's not like they're collector's items or anything. They're just old.

There are ways in which presidents remind me of characters in a video game. They are reduced to caricatures (think of the time it takes cast members on Saturday Night Live to find the right few mannerisms to imitate, and how those few things eventually become our own imitations), they have costumes (think of Obama's tan suit, the relaxed jeans of W at the ranch),

they are here to save the day with our help. They have strengths—
Clinton, in his first-ever campaign, wore holes in three different
pairs of shoes (think of how much energy, how many miles it
takes to wear holes in three pairs of shoes). They have weakness-
es. For most of them, it is power (think of Nixon), but Clinton's
were on displays for all to see, his failures of self dried on a blue
dress from the Gap, as ready for the Republicans to use against
him as if they'd read it in a walkthrough.

I suppose what I am writing about is failure: failures of
presidents, failures of video games, failures of my own. I don't
really know what happened to the friends with whom I played
NBA Jam for a few days in Colorado in the last spring of high
school. There is a way in which we could regard Clinton's failure
of self as the catalyst for what followed—the campaign, the elec-
tion, the recount, Iraq, Afghanistan, Katrina. Who knows. The
programmers spelled his name wrong—"Gugliotti" instead of
"Gugliotta." No big deal. A big deal.

16-bit was where it stopped for me. I played Goldeneye five
years after those few days in Colorado, and it was too much for
me. I ended up dizzy, nauseated. I couldn't play those games
long enough to get anything done. I own an Xbox and a Play-
Station, and when I do play games (briefly—no marathons, no
three pairs of shoes), I am frustrated by how protected I am, how
often the checkpoints rescue me from my own incompetence,
how I could start again a few steps back, learn from my mistakes,
recognize my patterns. No error, a clean shot, proceed to the
next save point. Nothing lost. No Bullets into Wizards, no Gugliotta into Webber, no Ford's Theater into a government building
into wreckage into historic site.

I want to tell you a story I don't tell people. In fourth grade,
I played on a basketball team with my friends—a fun thing, no

pressure. I was left-handed, but hadn't had my growth spurt, and I was deeply uncoordinated (previous sports and my positions therein: tee-ball/right fielder, soccer/fullback, those are where kids like me played).

I did not score baskets. I tried and I missed. In practice, I could do this, but on the court for a game, I could not make it happen.

In a late-season game (the last?), the opposing team's coach, unhappy with something, went on a tirade. The referee blew his whistle, made a T with his hands, but the coach continued ranting. The referee calmly added penalty shots to the technical, free throw upon free throw. I do not remember how long it to took for the other team's coach to burn out his fury, but when it was over, our team had an massive number of free throws to take. I don't remember the exact number. Let's say eight.

Our coach turned to me—me, who had not scored a point all season long, and now here it was, almost over—he turned to me and said "Colin, take the free throws."

Bless him for his kindness. My parents and sister were there, my friends were there, my friends' parents were there. I walked onto the empty court to meet the referee under the basket, who passed me the ball and blew his whistle.

I missed every one. I watched them bounce off the backboard, the rim. There was nothing I could do, no code to enter to transform me into Gugliotta or Clinton, I would never be on fire. I would gain a power. I would never level up. I missed every one. I am a middle-aged man, well-employed, happily married, satisfied with life, and every single day I think about shooting eight free throws that miss and fall onto an empty court.

[BRI]

CLEVELAND CAVALIERS

There is some beauty to be found in passiveness, in the moments before the tip-off, in how you try to influence the world around you as best as you can, but are still subject to the whims of chance, of what was supposed to happen.

There are some days when the basket seems like it is right in front of me, a wrist-flick away. I am always distracted by what is going on around me: the faces in the crowd, my teammates hunched over and staring at the floor. When you shoot from the corner you are closer to everything. The outside of the game can reach out and grab you, pull you toward something that you have no

11

recollection of—that the game can easily cease without you giving it permission.

I wish I could tell you that every single shot that didn't go in was unlucky: the ball bounced a certain way that it has never bounced before, the pass would've been perfect if a defender wasn't standing there. This is all false: I wasn't fast enough; I did not practice hard enough; my form was off; I was subject to crowding.

Mark Price might not have hit every shot he took, but you believed that every shot he took would eventually find the net. His best year, he made slightly less than one in two shots from the three-point line: god-like in the grand scheme of how this game works. He now teaches players how to shoot better—those point guards who are all flash and sizzle but no fundamentals. He teaches them to keep their elbows in, to use their good eye to guide the ball up and over. We demand every open shot to go in—that these are professionals who have done this action thousands of times; there is no excuse for an air ball, a brick.

This is a game in which the word *miracle* is tossed on the air without discretion—prayers heaved, shots bouncing every which way before rattling through the rim and to the floor. If it's not luck, it's prayer; it is impossible for it to be both. To believe that any of this is achieved secularly is an insult to the mystery of the universe.

The truth behind the mystery of faith is that you have to believe in something you have no tangible evidence for: the existence of something larger than who we are, the cathedral's dome being anything but flat. There are algorithms in place in the game, dictating that every player has the ability to make a shot count, that it can be affected from where they stand on the floor. Every video game has these tricks: bounce infinitely for infinite lives, press the right combination over and over to make your opponent stay down.

The key to faith is repetition. There needs to be a constant proving—something that can be seen and felt in succession, a breath that we can trust will always be there for us when we are doubled over. There is no such thing as having strong or weak faith; this is not something tangible. You believe or you do not.

After Brad Daugherty's back went out, he bought stake in a NASCAR team—a sport that involves memorization of tracks the drivers will see hundreds of times in one race, the same turns made over and over.

At my college, every team had a priest on it—ours a wiry shooting guard from Baltimore with a salt and pepper jump shot he could hit from the baseline. A year after I graduated, he passed away in his apartment building; his heart suddenly giving out. Before one game, during warm-ups, he hit five or six shots in a row from the same spot. We all laughed at how easy this game was with both God and luck on his side. He chided us for discrediting his abilities. He told us that God doesn't care if his shot goes in—that by explaining everything in the world away, we make the world vanish into a blur, a smudge on every miracle that cannot be made whole again.

[BRI]

GOLDEN STATE WARRIORS

In the game, all players are ambidextrous. They are all so perfectly balanced between their left and right sides that they do not give any of this a second thought. They are controlled by simple buttons: pass, shoot. You do one thing or you do the other. There is no option to switch hands, to curl around your defender, to surprise the opposition with a fake scoop, or a desperately flung ball towards the backboard with the opposite hand.

The game, however, is consistent in its randomness: Chris Mullin will drive and scoop with his right hand; he will rain three-pointers with his left-hand, just like in real life, both hands up in the air with one wrist pointed forward. When the court is flipped and the Warriors are shooting toward the left basket, the players are mirrored—Mullin leaving his right-hand dangling.

As I tried to learn the up and under—as I tried to find a natural shooting rhythm—I couldn't help but believe that I should be doing this all differently, that the ball should be in my right hand, that I should be steadying it with my left, that if only I could shoot the ball the way that I was intended it would find the bottom of the net more times than not. I was a glitch in the system, a check sum during warm-ups that did not correspond. My love of basketball comes from the need to rely on the entire body—in soccer, I did not know which foot to plant and which one to swing. When my father bought me my first baseball glove, it was for the wrong hand. I would catch the ball, only to take my hand out of the mitt to throw it back—a ceremony cut short by impracticality.

My trick is that I go left, always—I cannot get right even if I wished it would happen, if I willed anything. This is one of many things you can figure out about me while on the court—you will learn that you can out-run me, you can out-jump me. It will not be difficult. I have always gone left before I knew I always went left: I imagine these games now, even as I have gotten much older. I can picture certain small moments from playing in rec leagues and for my school—how the ball felt like a balloon in my hands, how far away the basket seemed, how my socks would bunch up in my sneakers, how I dribbled to the left, how I thrust the ball into the air with my left palm.

And yet I can't help believing that I am hard-wired to go right. How I was intended was breached: while in the womb, I started to hit the bottom of my mother's ribs with the top of my head, like an unfortunate swimmer who opts to surface underneath the dock. I was to be extracted, to be slid through the transverse cut in my mother's abdomen with a soft reboot. Instead, I was delivered naturally and forcefully by my right arm. I spent the first year of my life in a velcroed tan sling that held my chubby forearm at a pseudo-right-angle. Babies are supposed to be perfection—fat noses and miniature mouths. It isn't until they begin to stretch that they grow hideous. Hair grows steady in some places, unfertilized in others. Fingers swell before arms, leaving gigantic fists at the end of fatty tubes. Stomachs and heads grow large like viruses, legs stay stubby. When I would run, my forehead would lead me, one arm swinging like a one-footed duck treading water.

Magic Johnson famously said "When God made a basketball player, he just carved Chris Mullin out and said *this is a player,*"—as if Mullin wasn't birthed, he was created; appearing one day in a gym in Flatbush shooting free throws. That Mullin was crafted perfectly, beautifully, that people like him are not born with a chance of disaster, that everything arrives just as it should, that he does not believe that people are born like he was crafted, that there are moments where the game freezes, where the shot rattles: where a tone emits from the cabinet that remains long and dull until everything restarts—until we have to pull the plug from the wall.

EX•AG•GER•ATE
\ig-'za-jə-,rāt\
verb
past tense: exaggerated
represent (something) as being
larger, greater, better, or worse than
it really is
synonyms: overstate, overempha-
size, overestimate, magnify, amplify,
aggrandize, inflate

In this version of "exaggerated nature
of play," the inflated head would be
the first thing you notice, a grapefuit
where there should be a grape. Then
the boost, the ability to soar and
score, skip and dunk, like no time
before, like I had only imagined. The

INDIANA PACERS

PLAYER 2

[GOB]

overstated slams, the overemphasized jerks, the action amplified.

And that's what drew us to it, to you, our heads also over-sized, our energies similarly combustible, though not as well-utilized. And that's how we drew ourselves in our made-up world between that and this, between "he's on fire" and "my dad got fired." Mom and dad needed a moment, so whichever friend/cousin/neighborhood kid was around and I would leap into the driveway, miniature basketball already bouncing, broom stick in the other hand. To lower the goal down to seven-and-a-half feet.

We did what we could to exaggerate the crossovers and spins, alley-oops and succession of threes. If we missed, we didn't re-member. If we couldn't manage a 360 jam, for instance, we'd spin on our toes before the leap. And if a friend wasn't tall enough or happy in the inflated conditions, he wouldn't stay long, the we reduced to just the exaggerated me.

My one-on-none breakfast sandwich crumbs hormonal battle in the half-light, my blue-and-yellow striped curtains leaking in the cornfield sun. Joystick to tick away each second, shot clock and game clock, wall clock and mom's clock. It was time to go to school, of course, of course, but my boxers were still bare, one last impossible windmill, ball on fire as I eek away from the real—from the real life, the real B-team basketball practice wait-ing after a day of real biology and real study hall, lucky to be as-signed the basketball coach and not the algebra teacher, replays on low volume on the television above his desk. I chomped my semi-real bacon, and you were holographic, mid-air.

NA•TURE
\'nā-chər\
noun
1. the phenomena of the physical world collectively, including plants, animals, the landscape, and other features and products of the earth, as opposed to humans or human creations
2. the basic or inherent features of something, especially when seen as a characteristic of it
synonyms: essence, inherent/basic/essential qualities

And what was your nature, Reggie? Somewhat-to-really cocky, depending on the opponent. Cold-blooded shooter. Scrappy-to-annoying defender, depending on who we're asking. But the features they gave you didn't match, your speed quicker, the dunks intensified, even the way you released, not even close. Reggie Miller, I couldn't recognize you.

Some people don't believe in digitized likenesses, a camera to suck their soul and the body left empty. Many years later Tupac vibrating on a stage in Indio, CA. My paper mâché you in eighth grade art got me a C and then crumbled, only a photo taped to a middle school scrapbook remains. And at home, I could play as you, Reggie Miller, though your head the wrong-sized bulb, your arms somehow too skinny even for you, the hops impossible, the three-point kick gone. But it had to be you there, heating up and burning through my mornings, taking me late into the evenings, taking down Dominique and Ewing, Pippen and the others. Jordan elsewhere glowing. Shaq dusty in arcades across the Midwest. You were there, here, everywhere, Reggie Miller, even if it didn't quite look like you.

And back into the driveway, where I didn't have to recognize the self I didn't understand, my character undeveloped, wanting but not being—loving like my father, passionate like my mother, aggressive on the real basketball court like Derek. My essence was what the truck drivers and country moms heading into the city for the night's pork chops saw—a gangly body, slow and without a jump shot or the ability to dunk, unless of course I lowered the goal.

A shrieker my entire life, joy and pain, anger and a brand new basketball, I go WOOO, and that day it was for you, your BOOM BABY poster raffle prize for "giving my best" on the standardized test, my bubbling in the third box, then the first box, third box then first box, a second box for good measure, occasionally a fourth, but it was you, the real you, Reggie Miller, a three and a one, my education depended on. And it was worth the dedication, the repetition, that poster sprawled out in the boys' room, your feet higher than we could ever jump, John Starks not close enough. I went WOO over the other boys' jealousy.

You were at the trailer park arcade, the cobwebs overhead, the single square window we needed our tip-toes for, to look out and see if anyone was coming, as we cursed and sprawled out on the pool table, taking turns. Matt's turn to jam, and he chose you, of course, and you were there, as I made out with Molly for the first time, as I touched her real breasts for the first time, tucked in that cavernous seat of *Cruis'n USA*, the grunts and the three-balls firing like two fireworks at once.

And what are fireworks, really, Reggie Miller, but holograms, chemical likenesses of what we were all hoping? Whisked by Molly to join her on the shore, Fourth of July like the five before, my uncle and his former drinking buddies, all sober now, un-docking with each of their thousand dollar contributions, aerial shells and display tubes, taking turns buying the finale, every year ending in the explosion of an American flag. Where were you, Reggie Miller? Practicing, or wasting away pixel by pixel.

OF
\əv\
preposition
1. expressing the relationship between a part and a whole
2. expressing the relationship between a scale or measure and a value

You were a part, but there were always two. You and McKey. You and Smits. You and Schrempf. Depending on the controller one was holding. I didn't recognize you, Reggie Miller, when there was just the other Pacer part to battle the Knicks when I let John Starks slip past. And how did you measure yourself there, Reggie Miller? My head higher, larger, than the others, but the stat chart stays empty. The game played at ten-feet.

I'm a fake. Not good enough with the joystick. Not good enough with the actual ball. Like Iverson into a press conference crowd, practice was not my understanding. Jump shots until three a.m., not to become you, Reggie Miller, not to be at Market Square Arena one day hoisting a banner finally, but because my hands twitched if I ever stopped. Me versus the CPU and missing the bus, not to one day beat Matt or Jason, but because it was you, Reggie Miller, and it was me, and I could hardly recognize us, so I'd play until maybe I could.

But that was it, the *NBA Jam* dabbles, that was it for my

video game days. I never learned the easter eggs, never slicked up the floors, you and your opponents, Reggie, sliding across the court, never unlocked Bill Clinton. I never got to play as *Mortal Kombat* characters I can't name. Just with you, Reggie Miller, until I sold my Genesis for a skateboard.

PLAY
\plā\
verb
1. engage in activity for enjoyment and recreation rather than a serious or practical purpose
2. to take part in (a sport)
noun
1. activity engaged in for enjoyment and recreation, especially by children
2. the conducting of an athletic match or contest

My shoulders finally properly prop up my big head, and I've come to terms with never being able to dunk. Reggie Miller, what did you do today without the Pacers? California breeze and cheese pizza, a tiny rehearsal for something to televise. This whole time, I've sounded uncharacteristically serious, my hunt for a practical purpose to my childhood play. But there, the play, playing, *play with me, play against me*, like ghost whispers from the hall, this is how it's supposed to be. Even these days, alone at the courts, I still pretend I'm you, Reggie Miller, a 40-foot three-point attempt as the shot clock expires, a turn-around jumper and a finger wag to the empty sideline. The enjoyment of every shot going in even when it doesn't.

A diversion from that medical bill I refuse to pay, one of the last ways to relax without a beer in my hand, I'm enjoying myself here when I do these things. The goal doesn't lower, but who says a one-handed layup isn't its own form of a dunk? Who says my parents aren't cheering from the stands? Who says I'm not on fire? Hey, I can't recognize myself when I'm you, Reggie Miller, and who says that it's a bad thing, this inflated essence of amusement?

[BRI]

PORTLAND TRAIL BLAZERS

There is something beautiful to the idea of home court. When you play the game, there is no telling who is home and who is away: the crowd cheers and boos each team equally; their only rooting interest is that of spectacle. They are here to be amazed and do not care who wins or loses.

We built our own court in our driveway—a promise that was made to me after years of living in a house too small for all three of us: the house I grew up in, a small Cape Cod on the side of the road, a gravel driveway, an area where there is only slope and nothing level enough for a hoop. The apartment complex we lived in while our house was being built did not have a basketball court. It had a few tennis courts where I spent an August afternoon sweating; the only time I had ever played that game until I was much older, a once-off thing that ended with a plunge into the pool and the promise of popsicles. In the apartment complex parking lot, I would play hockey. I would take my stick and orange ball and slam it into the garbage dumpster; I would get the right angle down so that it would bounce back to my stick without rolling underneath my neighbors' cars, so I wouldn't have to get on my hands and knees—ruining my good pair of jeans—to coax the ball from out underneath mufflers, or, god forbid, stretch my elbow down into a storm drain.

Here, in the house with my own room with windows that look out to the horses to the south, a basketball court branching off the side of the garage, the only part of the long driveway paved over, the rest consisting of individual rocks, a placeholder for dirt.

My father and I painted the lines: we measured the length of the free throw line, the arc of the three-point spot. In the key, a shamrock for my father's alma mater: a splotch of green that quickly wore away whereas the white lines, although faded, still let us know where to shoot from. The arc would extend all the way to the left, though would disappear when it hit where the driveway met grass—that the grade of the land was not enough to hold ourselves level.

It was more that we had it, to be honest, that I was the kid with a basketball court in his backyard, although it was only cut in half—perfect for three-on-three, the other end of the court represented by the gray siding on our garage. I would like to say that I spent hours practicing—jump shots, the up and under, the bank-shot from the left. However, there was always something in the way: the ball being left out in the cold and getting too flat, the driveway being muddy after it had rained. If you missed to the right, you had to chase the ball down the hill into the woods—a long shot that hit rim was the worst nightmare: hands reaching under brambles, the fear of getting gashed open by a thorn.

The idea of the Trail Blazers is transitory. The team was denied its existence from being too far away from the NBA's home base—there was fear that it was simply too expensive for teams to make the long trip to Portland. The team was expected to fold during its first few years, especially after the ABA merger brought new teams to the league. Portland's most famous players are famous because they fell apart: the knees of Walton, and Bowie, and Oden coming off their hinges. Clyde Drexler, the face of the franchise, was always synonymous with Houston and left the Blazers to win a championship with the Rockets.

The night we christened the hoop, I shot ill-advised three pointers in hopes of making the first basket something beautiful. The ball would go bouncing into the darkness with every miss. I kept moving in closer until one finally went in: an ugly line drive of a shot that clanked off the backboard and rattled home. Not long after, I would quit playing basketball competitively, my body too slow and my skills too raw to be of any consequence.

The Trail Blazers' logo is that of constant motion: a pinwheel meant to symbolize ten players interweaving with each other— two masses moving in opposite directions. In some ways, it is meant to represent the fluidity of the game of basketball—everything working together to create some beautiful pattern. To me, it looks like the game passing by—the ball rolling into the thickets, fingers bloodied from the prickles, me somewhere off camera just watching.

[BRI]

DETROIT PISTONS

Here are the basketball courts of my youth. My middle school had two gyms: one titled "Old" and the other "New," although the New Gym had been around since well before I was born. The Old Gym was dim-lit and brown, the court dusty and the wood well worn from years of pivots and jump stops. The new gym was bright and almost yellow in its construction: blue walls and light-colored wood, a viking head painted at half-court. This is where my father played his games: where I sat on the sidelines and the scorer's table and flipped numbers, put ticks in soft pencil in a ledger book. I learned how to cuss here: a man taking a foul too hard,

accusations of it being intentional. We lash out because of fear—
that an ankle could've twisted and popped, though it didn't, that
someone could've snapped a forearm, but didn't. In the old gym
was where I was in my first fist fight—no punches thrown, just
a shove into stacked up bleachers after a hockey game, a stick
slashed against my wrists for no reason other than the fact that
I breathed too heavy, that I was ripe for the kill, that I wouldn't
dare strike back.

The most glowing character review of Barack Obama was
from his brother-in-law, then coach of Oregon State's men's basketball team: that he was fun to play with, that he was an unself-
ish player.

There was an outdoor court near the police station by my
house with stiff rims and crooked backboards—more apt for
layups than jump shots, the ball bouncing too high when dribbling due to the rubber court raised above the grass. To the right,
the chain-link fence of tennis courts, the occasional fuzzy neon
ball escaping on a poorly angled shot and finding its way into
our pick-up games. It was here where on a fast break, I sent a kid
crashing into the ground: I missed the block, but got all body, his
head cracking against the pipe that held the backboard in place,
all kids scattering in fear of being the one caught red-handed,
the ball bouncing and rolling away, untouched.

There are no fouls in *NBA Jam*, no solemn trip to the free
throw line, no bouncing of the ball before deep breaths and
perfect form. No blood, no foul. Shoving the player is legal and
your best form of defense: hit the player as soon as they start to
elevate toward the basket; to send them sprawling in an attempt
to jar the ball loose.

There were the courts in college: of pick-up ball, of walls
dropped down to separate games, to prevent a bleed-over from

one court to another. There was the punch swung after a box out, that I was taking the game too seriously, that I would just let a kid taller than me grab a rebound simply because he towered over me—his height preventing him from getting a good angle on my forehead, him promising to fight me in the parking lot after the game was over.

My father played against Bill Laimbeer in college; he graduated from Notre Dame the year after Laimbeer was drafted. My father always said he was the biggest asshole he ever played against.

The blacktop in Belgium that was constantly rain-slicked, the ball skidding off at raw angles, the long jump sandpit nearby which scattered silt into the key—our feet sliding out from under our bodies. I'd like to tell you a story of language being misconstrued, of Flemish being pronounced incorrectly, of culture shock leading to violence, but it was our own who fought: head down, barreling into the lane with nothing on the tongue but aggression, of not knowing how to leave things on the court.

There's something to be said about the character one has on a basketball court: I would vouch for people I played with—people I barely knew, folks I would see out at the bar. I would have some sort of kindred spirit with them. People would ask me what I thought of people and I would say *well, I played basketball with them*, as if this was a stamp of approval. In a way, it was.

The courts in Alabama—sweat-stained and warped from humidity—of a September birthday where a friend demanded he play despite too many drinks at lunch, of saying the wrong thing to the wrong stranger, of being punched in the face, of refusing to go home afterward, of him begging us to keep playing while we sat on the court in silent protest.

The game, in contrast, has one court: there are rumors that

there was another one based off of a fighting game—of blood and other worlds and never realms. This was partially true: a mock-up of the court did exist, but it was never accessible. The makers of the game wanted to disassociate it from violence— there is no room for blood or anger in the game, in basketball, in any of this.

I have stories that I tell more than other stories. There is that time that I went swimming in a lake with my parents. I was three years old. I don't remember a lot about being three, but I do remember that day and seeing an octopus peek its head out of the water and look at us. I swam to the shore immediately. "There's an octopus in the water," I told my parents. If I knew anything at three years old it was how to identify animals. "Octopi can't swim in freshwater lakes," my parents told me and laughed. They thought I was making a funny joke. People often think I am joking when I'm not. There is something about the cadence of my Minnesotan accent.

MINNESOTA TIMBERWOLVES

PLAYER 2

[TLC]

Something about the way I say *boat* or *bag* or *Minnesota*.

Sometimes there are certain bodies where we do not expect these bodies. I was three in 1991, the year I saw the octopus in the lake. I did not expect to see the octopus in the lake, but there it was. I was three in 1991 and my dad had season tickets to the Minnesota Timberwolves. Another story I like to tell is the story of the Minnesota Timberwolves as werewolves. People laugh the same way that my parents laughed at the story of the octopus in a freshwater lake. They think I have a bad misunderstanding of what bodies can do. They laugh at the word *werewolves*. They think that I am making a joke. Jokes are stories that make people uncomfortable, so maybe I am joking. But I did see an octopus in the lake that day. Who is to tell a body what it can do and what it can't?

One time my father, my brother, and I tried to climb a mountain. Sometimes I talk about metaphorical mountains, but this was a literal mountain. None of us had ever climbed up a mountain before. The path was only accessible at certain times of the year. None of us were sure if this was that time and we had only four bottles of water. We passed other hikers who had full backpacking gear and walking sticks. We were walking only with our feet. In my family, we have chronic foot problems. Plagued with falling arches and sprained ankles and fractured bones.

We did not make it to the top of the mountain. This is not a metaphor either. We passed the tree line. There was snow on the ground. I said, "What a beautiful view, we should turn around now before we run out of water." My brother Kevin said, "We should keep going; I will drink the snow."

My brother was born in 1994, the year that the Target Center hosted the NBA All-Star game and the year that Isaiah Rider won the Slam Dunk Contest. My brother Kevin doesn't remem-

ber this. When I ask him about the early years of the Timberwolves he says, "Was that before Kevin Garnett?" All timelines
for the Minnesota Timberwolves relate back to someone named
Kevin.

The entire way back down the mountain, my brother Kevin
explained to my father and me all the ways in which our bodies
had failed us. We were not driven enough, he said. We had not
spent enough time conditioning our bodies to climb a mountain. We were from Minnesota. What did we know about climb-
ing mountains?

I am not good at lifting weights or opening doors or running
quickly. We all have our flaws. The Minnesota Timberwolves are
historically bad at playing basketball. We are each trying to fix
these things in our own ways.

I started competing in triathlons when I was 23. When I first
told my father that I wanted to do a triathlon he laughed at me.
My body is not the right type of body for an athlete. My other
hobbies include watching television, eating pizza, and knitting.
My body on a triathlon course is like an octopus in a freshwater
lake. I wanted to do a triathlon because I thought it would transform my body. I wanted to be something that I wasn't. I wanted
to do things I thought my body couldn't do. A friend once told
me that people in Minnesota are the hardest workers because
people in Minnesota have to live through the winter each year.
To live in Minnesota is to know that life is hard.

The Minnesota Timberwolves started playing basketball in
1989, 29 years after the departure of the Minneapolis Lakers. The
movie *Teen Wolf* was released in 1985. The early Timberwolves
were nothing like a wolf playing basketball. Each year, I try to
make myself more like a triathlete. Each year, the Minnesota Timberwolves try to make themselves more like basketball players.

My first triathlon was a sprint distance on Lake Minnetonka. People who are not from Minnesota know the name Minnetonka. Minnetonka Moccasins and Minnetonka of *Purple Rain*. Rumor has it the waters are purifying. I finished, but not quickly. I developed a foot injury along the way. A month later I did the Heart of the Lakes triathlon. My father referred to the race as "homegrown" the distance dictated by the landscape. Many people believe that it never gets warm in Minnesota, that, despite its proximity to Milwaukee or Chicago, it stays buried under the ice for the entirety of the year. On the day of the triathlon, it was 93 degrees outside. Wetsuits were banned from the competition. Instead of just drinking at the water stations I dumped cups over my head. I lost sight of everyone on the course with the exception of one lone man alternating between running and walking in front of me. I was running, but barely. A flock of geese nearly attacked at one point. A man in a golf cart drove by and asked if I wanted some water. "No," I said. He circled back again and again until I took the bottle. "I was getting worried," my father said when I finally finished. "It was a tough race," I said.

I try to combat the faults of my body through constant exercise and by eating spinach. I watched a lot of *Popeye the Sailor Man* as a small child and it taught me the ways a body can transform through eating greens. I want my muscles to swell the way that Popeye's did after he downed all those cans. I look for signs that the spinach has fused with my body: a greenish tint to my skin, a bulge in my arms, but I remain the weak person I have always been. I am trying to turn my body into a vegetable, something fueled by the sun. Becoming spinach seems equally as attainable as becoming an athlete. I feel uncomfortable with the term. I feel the need to hedge my activities. Yes, I do this, but I do it slowly. Yes, I do this, but it is nothing like the way that you picture it being.

The answer for the Minnesota Timberwolves lay not in spinach, but in apples. The Honeycrisp apple was designed in the 1960's at the Horticultural Research Center at the University of Minnesota. One of the goals of the research center was to breed apples that could withstand the harsh climate of Minnesota winters. The Honeycrisp apple is a hybrid of two different types of apples. Together, they are more resilient than the previous types of apples. The Honeycrisp apple can survive the tough Minnesota winter.

It is one thing to put two apples together in order to make another type of apple. It is quite another to take a human body and a wolf body and make those the same body. It is uncertain whether the movie *Teen Wolf* came first or whether it was a wolf that was suspiciously like a teenager and played basketball that inspired the movie. Something about a chicken and an egg, except that it was scientists who took the egg and turned it into a chicken.

After a long workout, I drink a protein shake. It's supposed to help with recovery. My protein powder is made from grass-fed cows. It doesn't say which part of the cow, and I imagine them, their strange cow bodies, put into a blender whole. We are constantly consuming other things in order to make these things a part of ourselves. This idea is not so strange. I am five bananas a week. I am 14 eggs. I am seven turkey sandwiches. I drink the powder, but I do not become a cow. I am still human. I wait for my muscles to grow, but they are static. I flex and push upon the squish in my arms. I swim laps in the pool like it does something.

The Honeycrisp apple was designed in the 1960's, but it was not released until 1991. The process of hybridization is a long one. The apples are given numbers instead of names. Before the

Honeycrisp was a Honeycrisp it was the MN 1711. Before the Honeycrisp reached its status as a desired fruit, the University of Minnesota declared it a failure and slated it to be discarded. Not all apples can be good apples. Not all humans can be wolves who play basketball.

MN 32 was named Christian Laettner. Christian Laettner was named MN 32. They had a whole team of subjects on the field that year, but Laettner was the most promising. They began testing him in the field in 1992. Laettner is most famous for his last second, back-to-the-basket jump shot during the 1992 NCAA tournament during the East Regional Finals between Duke and Kentucky. Because of Laettner's shot, Duke beat Kentucky with a score of 104-103 and went on to beat Michigan to become the champions of the tournament. It was after this that he was drafted to the Wolves. To become a professional basketball player is to put certain demands on the body. You cannot say no when a professional basketball franchise asks if you want to be a wolf and slaps a number on your back. You cannot say no when a scientist sticks a needle in your arm and says, "This will help."

My brother Kevin was a promising athlete. He was on the swim team and the cross country team. He ran his first half marathon at the age of 12 and went straight from the race to a swim meet. He started competing in triathlons at the age of 14. The announcer on the course said, "Look at this 14-year-old up in the front with the professionals." One time while watching a 2013 NBA Finals game, my brother said, "Lebron just doesn't have what it takes to be a winner. He doesn't have enough drive. If I were Lebron, I would work so much harder than he does." My brother stopped competing in triathlons when he was 18 years old. He's had a broken arm, a broken wrist and he fractured his collarbone while biking. His body remains thin. He still looks like an athlete, but he wasn't even able to run in college. "I didn't drink enough milk as a child," he says when I asked him about his bones.

"A disappointment," my father says when I mention Laettner's name. My father can barely remember who Laettner was. "Was that before Garnett?" he asks. All timelines for the Minnesota Timberwolves relate back to someone named Kevin. Despite all his promise, MN 32 was declared a failure. They made him more than human. They made him a wolf and his body still failed him when he reached the summit. This is a metaphorical summit. The Minnesota Timberwolves have rarely reached the playoffs. Laettner was traded to the Atlanta Hawks after that. Don't even ask if he was turned into a literal hawk. Everyone knows humans can't fly.

MN 21 and MN 42 were more successful subjects. 21 and 42 were variations of the same wolf. They both originated as Kevin, but one was Kevin Garnett and the other Kevin Love. These subjects were named Kevin after the longtime General Manager Kevin McHale. It might seem like a coincidence, it might seem like they were named Kevin because that is what their parents named them and that is what the scientists want you to think. People are uncomfortable with the idea of lab experiments. People don't like it when different genes are combined. If word got out there would be calls for GMO labels on basketball players. "GMOs are bad for your basketball team," people would say. "Don't you want players who are organic?"

Throughout both Garnett and Love's careers on the Timberwolves, announcers and critics lamented that they were not playing for better teams. The Timberwolves were not worthy of their talent. What these commentators failed to realize was that the Timberwolves made them what they were. That once they joined the team they became the hybrid of a good apple and a better apple to become the best apple. It was not their fault they were stuck on a team with some bad apples. Not all hybridizations are successful hybridizations. Perfection comes slowly and at a cost.

The question remains, how does an octopus hide in a freshwater lake and how do wolves hide on a basketball court? How can there be all of these Wolves walking around in the NBA, showering with human NBA players, letting their giant Wolf bodies crash into those players that are still only human. How can they hide in plain sight like that? Like a single Honeycrisp hiding in a bag of Red Delicious.

When I first started running I was worried people would see me. "You're not a runner," they would say in my imagined fantasy. "Take off those shoes and that ankle brace. Stop posturing," they would continue. No one has ever said this to me. I watch my figure in the reflections on buildings. I flex what muscles I have in the mirror. In the water I pretend I am a fish or an Olympic swimmer, species that are not as far apart as they seem. The bodies of Olympic swimmers are disproportionate. Their arms are too long, their feet too wide. My body is disproportionate too, but it all the wrong ways. My hips are too big and my feet too narrow. I am self-conscious about the size of my thighs and the inability to flex my back as I do the butterfly. I am not good at imitating things outside of myself.

Isaiah Rider was drafted straight out of college by the Wolves in 1993. Rider was supposed to be fresh blood for the Wolves. He was featured on two versions of *NBA Jam* with Christian Laettner and he won the Slam Dunk Contest in 1994 with a dunk called "The East Bay Funk Dunk." He later recorded a track on the rap album *B-Ball's Best Kept Secret* called "Funk in the Trunk." Rapping has never been basketball's best-kept secret. Every basketball player knows this, particularly on nights when the full moon hits, when all of the Wolves players claim to be out on injury. The problem with injecting fresh blood into the Wolves is that the Wolves inject their full moon fever right back.

Rider did not take well to being a Wolf. This happens sometimes. Problems with the transfusion. A rejected experiment. He was with the team for three seasons before joining Portland Trail Blazers. He might have been okay. He might have moved on, except some things are impossible to move on from. His basketball career ended in 2001. In 2007 he was sentenced to seven months in jail for cocaine possession. This might be unrelated. There are people who have been arrested for cocaine possession that have never been Wolves at all. There are a lot of coincidences in the NBA. There are also no coincidences in the NBA.

During Minnesota Timberwolves games, it is custom to howl during the other team's free throws. When I attend Wolves games, I do this wholly and with all my heart for I am an enthusiastic sports fan. This is supposed to be a distraction technique and it is a distraction, but what it's distracting is not the player who is shooting the ball. It's distracting from the way that Minnesota players, whenever their home court is threatened, howl at the moon to stake claims on their territory and sprinkle a little urine around the boundaries of the court.

I have never done an Ironman triathlon. After persistent injuries my doctor advised me to only do sprint distance competitions because my body is not resilient. In defiance, I continue to do Olympic distance races. In 1870 a scientist mistakenly claimed that spinach had an iron value ten times higher than it actually does. This mistake was not rectified until the 1930s, leading to decades of false belief in the iron properties of spinach. Thus, despite my greens intake, I am not yet an Ironman. I remain wholly myself. I have mantras that I repeat when I run. I tell myself I am stronger for constantly battling insecurities about my body. I tell myself it's harder for an octopus to swim where it does not belong.

It took 30 years for the Honeycrisp apple to be put on the market. The Wolves have only been in existence for 25. "We need to give up on the Timberwolves," my brother Kevin tells my father. "The Twins are the Minnesota team of the future." Yet, despite all the failures, we persist. I continue to run six days a week. I bike and I swim through exhaustion. People marvel. "You're the hardest working person I know," they say, but they never tell me I'm the best. My brother Kevin reads articles about the Timberwolves on the daily. He looks at numbers and stats. He tastes the apples on the tree and evaluates them for their goodness. He will know when the Wolves have enough drive, when they can climb up the metaphorical mountain. "Kevin will never forget about that time we didn't climb up that mountain," my father says and laughs as we look over the freshwater lake filled with octopi. It's a joke, but it's not a joke. You never forget when you see an octopus in the lake. You never forget when you see a wolf on the basketball court.

[BRI]

ATLANTA HAWKS

I shoot baskets in a university gymnasium two hundred miles from where the Omni once stood. I keep to myself: I share a court with no one, I put my keys on the bench just past the sideline; I fill my water bottle to the top.

Basketball is a younger man's game; it is a game in which knees go quicker the older one gets, it is a game for bodies that have not yet begun to break down thanks to the perpetual off-season that I have lead ever since I stopped playing competitively. I have not played in a pick-up basketball game in over four years. Even when I would be considered too old and creaky by professional standards, I played twice a week with others my age or older. We would miss more than we would make, but we knew each other's game: watch the jump-step on that one, keep an eye on the sudden crossover, get a hand in his face from out there.

The year the game is released, Dominique Wilkins wins comeback player of the year. This award is a backhanded compliment—the idea that things were so awful, and yet somehow it was all overcome, that it was entirely unexpected. In Nique's case, he ruptured his Achilles' tendon, missing ten months. As with most comeback players, they do not stay back; they flare up brightly before slowly dimming back out to ash.

I knew a Dominique of legend; I would watch a documentary on Larry Bird at my grandfather's house at least once a month. There, Nique and Bird did battle: a Game 7 duel in '88 when Nique's Hawks came up short, despite him going 19-of-23 from the floor. Four years later, Nique is on the decline, though perfectly preserved here: his ability to dunk never suffering despite years removed from the height of his power.

As a Celtics fan, I was excited when Wilkins joined my team in 1994, because I did not understand how age works. I did not know that 35 is too old to be playing basketball, that Dominique is the same age in the game that I am now, that my knees start to go shortly after warm-ups. I thought he was magic, a name that transcends age, not knowing that the body breaks down, that jumping that was once natural becomes a chore.

But here, in the game, we remember Nique as we remember most legends: as unstoppable beings at the height of their powers, dunk rating maxed out, flying around the court even without the use of turbo. There is something beautiful about how a game can capture the essence of something—when we watch a film, we know that the actors existed on a different plane, that they are stuck somewhere in time, that the world rotates without them and shifts our perception of every actress. However, when we play a videogame, our nostalgia kicks in—we only remember the good: how Nique was robbed in the 1988 Slam Dunk Contest, how he slashed through the lane and drove the ball home with the force of a hurricane.

When I am shooting baskets, alone, chasing after every miss, young bucks will approach me, asking if I want to *run threes, run fives*. I often tell them I'm just wrapping up. In the grand scheme of things, I am—I am always a few more shots missed short from taking my ball and going home. Other days, I tell them that I'm too old for this, that they want to play a young man's game, that my time is better spent trying to defeat myself in games I make up in my head: how many times in a row can I make a shot from this corner, how many times can I make it around the world?

Now, I exist only as Kevin Willis, teammate of Wilkins and Augmon, who never made the grade. He was never worth the pixels to turn him immortal. Willis played until he was 44 and an All-Star in Nique's absence—longevity versus mythology. There is no time for age if you are not also legend.

I am here to tell you that I am ready for comeback, if even for a moment, if even for a breath that lasts long enough for the world to ask where I have come from, and where I am going. This is how I wish to be remembered: not at the peak of all that I am, but in the quiet moments afterward; I am spinning in the air, arms outstretched, ready to be underestimated. Find me here, aware of my body, keeping pace with young legs. Find me moving at less than full speed, scared of burning through. Seek me out, weakened by time and fate, but strong in will.

In my heart, the Phoenix Suns are the eponymous celestial organ of *NBA Jam*. The game was released for SNES in 1994, the year after Charles Barkley joined the Suns and the team made it to the Finals against the Chicago Bulls, who were sporting Scottie Pippen and a man named Michael Jordan. That was IRL, though; no one can play as Michael Jordan or against Michael Jordan in *NBA Jam*, because Michael Jordan, not the NBA, owns Michael Jordan. The same went for Shaquille O'Neal and Gary Payton, although M. Jordan and G. Payton later commissioned, for their personal pleasure, a version of *NBA Jam* in which they were a team. And

PHOENIX SUNS

PLAYER 2

[MTP]

maybe, for four stunted video game quarters, M. Jordan felt like the rest of us, his A resulting in jumps no higher and his Turbo no faster than any other player's special powers on that virtual court. I bet he was pissed.

It makes me feel bad that I'm supposed to be talking about the Suns, but then I get stuck on the Bulls. It makes me feel bad because that's how it happened in real life, too—the Bulls outshining the Suns. It's like when Farrah Fawcett landed that two-hour documentary on NBC that chronicled her slow death by cancer, and it seemed implicit that the un-filmed epilogue would be Farrah's death itself, making the whole enterprise this big fat wake for her life. And she wasn't even dead yet—just wait till she was dead! And then she died the same day as Michael Jackson. All that buildup for nothing. That's what it is to be outshone.

The worst thing about being outshone is how polarizing it is: even if you are just one point behind your opponent, as in the case of the Suns against the Bulls in Game 6 of the 1993 Finals, you are the loser. It doesn't matter how many times you had to be the winner to get to the place where you are suddenly a loser. The only consolation is that to be outshone implies that you made it just a little harder for the shinier party to do his outshining. But mostly you are forgotten. Ricky Bobby's daddy was right: *If you're not first, you're last!* That motto is like the lyrics of a love song: twee but true, because if you try to intellectualize the concept, you will sound like a moron.

The 1992-93 Phoenix Suns were the most explosive iteration of the franchise since 1977. In fact, it doesn't seem accidental that *NBA Jam* captures, in its boxy-graphicked way, the Suns at the moment the entire team was *woken up* Rip Van Winkle-style from their deep snoozery since that 1976-77 season. *NBA Jam* preserves, in a video game jar, the pinnacle of the Phoenix Suns, a pinnacle unsurpassed until the Steve Nash era another R.V. Winkle nap later.

If you are a visual person, go to the Wikipedia page for *NBA Jam* and take a look at the duos representing each team. You do not even have to be literate to see that the vast majority of the reps do not change. Static, unchanging, the worst state of being I know of. And then the Phoenix Suns are down there with a different combination of all-stars at pretty much every turn of the console. That's mostly because Charles Barkley got his own game called *Barkley Shut Up and Jam!* and so legally couldn't appear in *NBA Jam* anymore, at which point Dan Majerle's likeness replaced his.

But in my mind, the Suns' changing *Jam* roster has so much to do with what a dynamic team the Suns are and have been and ever will be. They're so dynamic that the seismic waves of their dynamism are registered in the 16-bit world. The way they were later noted as one of the more *touch-bonded* teams during the 2009-10 season seems also to suggest this dynamism, this movement and literal hands-on approach that keeps them vital. Those who think that *vital* is the wrong word to describe the Suns can be described in one word themselves: fair-weather. Watching a team just because they win all the time is like marrying a supermodel. You date those women, but don't you marry them.

Anyway, the most touch-bonded teams are the winningest ones. In one game, Steve Nash gave 239 high fives. The Lakers of the same season are noted to be the most physically demonstrative, and it's telling that they are the team the Suns came up against in that year's Western Conference finals. The Celtics were the second touchiest team in the league at the time, and they won the Eastern Conference finals. I imagine the Suns' *Jam* roster being like so many players tagging each other onto and off of the court, all getting time, playing like a team.

There's a way that wine exhibits characteristics particular to the place it was produced. We call this *terroir*. It's something in the air, something in the earth. And I have to feel like something similar is going on with the Suns. I know I've talked about them in terms of a diptych between the 1992-93 and 2009-10 teams, but those specific rosters illuminate patterns in the franchise that suggest that whatever's in the Phoenix air is the vitality I see in the franchise as a whole.

The year before *NBA Jam* was released for SNES was the season that the Suns returned from an 0-2 deficit in the Western Conference finals to upset the Seattle SuperSonics for the title. (Gary Payton, too rich and/or talented to appear in *NBA Jam*, was playing point guard for the SuperSonics at the time.) Then, in taking on the Chicago Bulls at the Finals, the Suns led Game 3 into triple-overtime. The only other time in the history of the NBA Finals that triple-overtime has occurred was in 1976, and that was a Suns game, too.

They played with such determination that when Charles Barkley famously told Michael Jordan that it was destiny for the Suns to win the Finals, it seemed more like a premonition than his ego. Nobody remembers what Michael Jordan said back, because that year was the second championship of Three the Hard Way. The Bulls outshone the Suns once again.

Destiny. The sheer overuse of that word, especially in this country, leads me to try to recover its original meaning, to see if it's possible that Charles Barkley wasn't actually wrong, like maybe there's an alternative definition of *destiny* that he was using. Self-awareness, after all, is the best thing after sheer, unassailable ego reinforced—and earned—through wins and wins and wins (see: Michael Jordan, LeBron James, Kobe Bryant).

But there's no alternative definition of *destiny*. Barkley was just wrong. A real human being, sunk in error like the rest of us.

Barkley emphasized such fallibility, actually, in a 1993 Nike commercial for which he wrote the text himself (!): "I am not a role model." Barkley argued that "the media demands that athletes be role models [but] what they're really doing is telling kids to look up to someone they can't become, because not many people can be like we are. Kids can't be like Michael Jordan."

Oh but *Charlie*, can't they try to be like you? That triple-overtime against M.J., et al, in Game 3 of the 1992-93 conference finals! Your own triple-double in the game after that! Playing six games in that series before the Suns went down! Tell me that kind of tenacity isn't worth teaching kids about. Tell me that pulling out those kinds of stats against the greatest NBA player playing for the third-winningest franchise in history isn't a role to be modeled.

And the irony of playing as the Suns in *NBA Jam* is that no team and no player is any better than the others, as if in being rendered in two dimensions, all talent is flattened, too. Also, pretty much the best players in the league are absent: Barkley, Jordan, Payton, O'Neal. It's like, what's the point? That flatness is replaced, of course, by the wild moves the game allows: mid-court threes that might as well be layups, rebounds high enough to clear the heads of the other weirdly tall players—not to mention the superpowers. People get mad at Barbie for being all out of proportion, but they obviously haven't played *NBA Jam*, and that is actually modeled on extant people.

I have this theory about athletes, and about other stupidly talented people: We all have a certain amount of Brain Juice. Some people are born with more of it than others, but you don't even have to be born with more, really, to be the best at something; you just have to be able to send all of your Brain Juice to that particular talent. The only drawback is that it's like blood to a penis: there ain't much more juice to be shared throughout the land. So you watch people like Michael Jordan, whose on-court, very personal taunts have been known to ruin other players' confidence for all time (he once told Muggsy Bogues to "take the shot you fucking midget" and Bogues aired it and says his J has never recovered). Or people like Tracy Austin, the junior tennis star who, at the tender age of nineteen, "quickly accepted that there was nothing [he] could do about [his shattered leg]." What's with these people?

Brain Juice. Brain Juice is with these people, but it's only congealing around their mad talent. So there's no room for considering your effect on others, and there's no room for an existential crisis when your livelihood disintegrates before half the people your own age have lost their virginity. To fully acknowledge these consequences takes Brain Juice that is just not available.

But every once in a while, you get athletes who have more Brain Juice than most humans, period. These are the athletes we love to love, not love to hate. People like Steve Nash, who opened a children's hospital in South America. People like Charles Barkley, whose avuncular spunk in his commentary makes it okay for *the rest of us* to get into watching basketball. People like Grant Hill, who owns a substantial collection of African-American art. People like Kevin freaking Johnson, who during a 1991 All-Star game wore Suns teammate's Mark West's no. 41 as a way of honoring West for his stoicism and strength on court, especially during the 1993 Finals—a fact that had to be deduced by analysts, because Johnson verbalized nothing. Mr. Johnson currently serves at the mayor of Sacramento, California.

These men are too good to keep their Brain Juice in the places that might make them the best at basketball.

The Phoenix Suns of *NBA Jam* represent the same wash they got swept up in the year before the game's release. The Suns show up—really show up—in their games against the Bulls, but it doesn't matter; they lose. They show up in *NBA Jam*, but it doesn't matter; they're no better than anyone else. The game is like socialism, plus everyone gets superpowers. I can't imagine a more effective combination for kids who couldn't ball in real life, kids like me who were so scrawny they had to shoot free-throws granny-style just to make it to the rim, kids who applied the concept of button-mashing to their athletic endeavors and then choked at every golden moment presented to them. Here is a game those kids can win, because the second chances don't stop coming.

But what makes the Suns special is that they don't win, that they remain—probably forever—the underdogs. There's no good place for them to win. But Jesus H. Christ do they show up.

[BRI]

BOSTON CELTICS

My father woke me up one morning to tell me that Reggie Lewis was dead. It was the first person I remember dying after I understood what dying meant: there had been goldfish, there had been neighbors, grandparents of friends.

I remember my father's voice when he told me: surprise above sincerity. This is not the voice he used when my cousin died: a definitive statement—*is dead* instead *of died*, something that will live with us forever instead of something that happened.

When you lose in the game, it restarts. You are kicked back to the splash screen. You put your quarters in. You select your team again. The same thing happens if you win: there is nothing beyond the world of the game, no post-game interviews, no showers that must be taken, no driving home on the team bus. You begin again.

The game keeps track, though. You must know that every time you enter your initials you are being watched. The game tallies your losses. It tells you the teams that you have defeated and the ones that you have yet to take down.

When you defeat all of the teams, you are rewarded with a photograph of two cheerleaders standing on a basketball court in front of the arcade cabinet. The photograph changes to the cheerleaders popping a bottle of champagne, one of them turning away as the alcohol sprays straight up in the air.

The game promises you that a greater challenge waits. It encourages you to play on.

The game is over, however. There is no grand finale, no super team that descends from the ceiling, no ghosts of superstars past that challenge you to a final game. You are promised something larger, and yet there is nothing left to do. The game resets.

Reggie Lewis died while shooting baskets in a gymnasium near his house. My cousin died in his garage, right next to the hoop that we would play on over the summer when we were tired of doing cannonballs into the pool, or playing the game in the basement.

I have missed more shots than I've ever made. I have hit nothing but backboard. I have shot the ball long so it bounces straight back to me off of the back iron. I have missed the rim entirely and looked around to make sure that no one has seen. The game resets, a blank slate. It is not flashy, it does not change its dynamics, and it does not make you do anything but the game: no shooting of aliens, no vanquishing of ghosts. It does not make you do anything but agree to its terms, which do not deviate, no matter how much we believe that the game is rigged against us. You will shoot until you miss. You will miss, and you will miss, and you will miss.

[BRI]

UTAH JAZZ

There is a belief that your house is always your house, that when you walk into your bedroom, you should never think of the lives that existed there before you: ghosts in the carpet, an indentation in the floor where the bedposts were. Names are like this too: if you enter your initials for record-keeping there is no one else that could come close to that combination of letters. We unlock ourselves through words. A few select glyphs can mean something, can be something that we are known to strangers as, that these letters are our birthright. You wish to believe that you are alone: no moments where you can be picked up and moved into another body, another house with different walls, unpainted baseboards, upstairs rooms where no children sleep.

This is how we justify the renaming of ourselves—that we will not have the strength to carry the weight of our fathers, of how we must call ourselves something different and strange altogether; that we spend hours trying to live up to the names that existed before us, but also do our best to separate ourselves: the same note, but a different octave.

At my grandparents house I would watch the film *Hoosiers*, about a high school basketball team in Indiana who overcame all odds to win the state championship. Upon arriving in Indianapolis for the championship, the players are overwhelmed by the size of the arena. Their coach takes out a tape measure and has the students measure the length of court, the height of the basket, to prove to them that it is the same dimensions of their gym back home, that the game remains the same regardless.

The game has much iteration: versions with new players, cartridges that you can bring home instead of fishing through your parents' pockets for quarters. The game shifts in certain ways: it looks less impressive, players are replaced, logos are updated, but it remains the same regardless of whether it is played in the confines of friends' basements or in the open air of a pizza parlor.

The joke is that despite the game remaining the same, whether in Indiana, or New Orleans, or in the gymnasiums where my father made free-throws—where I missed them badly—there is no jazz in Utah. There is no sadness written about salt lakes and mountains, crisp air and beehives. If there are sad songs to be written, they are not that kind of blues: the ones that taste like silt and swamp, of displacement, of existence, of knowing that you will die in the same town where you were born.

My father tells a story of being offered a job in the swamplands of Louisiana; that we would've moved there when I was five, that all I would've known would be completely different. I would develop an accent, I would say my name differently than I do now: a slurring together of consonants rather than an emphasis on the different syllables—like *brine*, like pickling my old life in a Ball jar.

Karl Malone, like the Jazz, is from Louisiana. Karl Malone, like the Jazz, does not fit his nickname: the Mailman, named as such for his consistency. Malone did not care about return to sender stamps; he did not keep track of what names no longer live at each of the houses.

On the court, I am called a lot of things—none of which are my name: the product of pickup games with strangers. They call me *Big Man, Boss Man*, the color of my shirt. I am never the first, and I know this: these names are universal. Every player with a heavy step and a scooping hook takes on more multitudes than they contain. I am among a long line of nomenclature, calling for the ball on the post, never winning the big one.

In the game you cannot create yourself—it cannot be you running point, making shots you could never take. They will never call your name as you grab a rebound, as you attempt a quick put-back. They will not announce your hometown, your height, how old you have gotten. When the game resets, it forgets your name and where you have been. It will ask you who you are, what day you were born. It will not ask you what house you have lived in your entire life. You cannot take credit for any of this. You cannot exist anywhere outside of where the game believes you belong.

The Seattle SuperSonics no longer play at KeyArena. They no longer play at all, in fact. Their logo and their colors are now trophies for the marauding Investment Conglomerate that moved the franchise to Oklahoma. KeyArena is still nestled there in Seattle, though, an odd little bomb shelter of a building. And befitting a venue built for the Century 21 Exposition that also brought the Space Needle to the city, KeyArena was the site of America making one more ignoble step toward the space age it has long pursued: in July of 2014, KeyArena first played host to professional video gaming. "The International,"

SEATTLE SUPERSONICS

PLAYER 2

[EPI]

a \$10-million Dota 2 tournament was contested amongst a globally-sourced menagerie of Nerds held aloft on a giant stage in the stadium. Where years before fans of all ages and backgrounds sat and watched basketball played at an infinitely unreachable level, Dota fans now sat watching their nerdy peers play a game they had also mastered on some algorithmically-lesser level. Professional broadcasters sat in front of their own bank of computers, directing virtual cameras over a computer-rendered battlefield. The finals were broadcast live on ESPN2.

Video game competition was considerably different when *NBA Jam* was released in 1993; then, lining up to challenge the reigning arcade rat-king was the nearest approximation of *esports*. The insidious appeal was essentially the same, though: here was something you could be among the best at without committing hours to anything other than having fun. Video game broadcasting technology was considerably different, too, which is to say: it was non-existent. Still, for some unenunciated reason, my best friend Conor and I felt it necessary to preserve our jamming-and-slamming exploits for future generations. His family's acquisition of a new TV meant the device hierarchy rotated one of those miniature, precariously-rectangular TV-and-VCR combination boxes into his control. Our immediate reaction was *why* wouldn't *we record ourselves beating the entire challenge ladder of* NBA Jam? An impossible question to answer, we quickly concluded, and we went about hooking up his Super Nintendo.

As next-door neighbors and best friends, there was an inevitable limit to competing against each other. Every basketball-based cartridge we could find had been plugged in between us at one point or another (shout-out to Bill Laimbeer's Combat Basketball for an especially innovative league mode). With a lifetime series score of *n* to *n±1*, coming up with new challenges was a necessity. We had stumbled onto what would come to be known as a *compstomp* among today's real-time strategy types. It was the pixelated equivalent of what we did on sunny Saturday mornings in Conor's driveway: playing 2-on-1 against his shirt-less, sweat-drenched dad with a fresh pack of Topps basketball cards on the line. We wanted to defeat the computer in a historic fashion, to the degree that might justify having a video tape of said stomping. This was a ridiculous exercise then; now, with people viewing weeks-old replays of games on Twitch just to glean a gameplay tip or two, it sounds almost reasonable. But we weren't honing the meta-game chops necessary to increase our matchmaking tier: we were in pursuit of perfection. We wanted three digits on our scoreboard and no positive integers on the computer's. We wanted to average 50 points apiece as if a pair of digital Wilt Chamberlains—perhaps one would have palette-swapped hair to avoid any confusion. We wanted to solve *NBA Jam* the way computers have solved checkers.

The prerequisite of the flawless *NBA Jam* performance was perfect defense. Scoring could barely be said to be a challenge with the advent of anti-gravity dunks and neon turbo shoes (is it the shoes?! it probably is the shoes). But most characters in *NBA Jam* were precursors of Carmelo Anthony: effortless, dynamic, incisive offense, with not a measurable trace of the fundamental tenets of defense. Once we had the ball there was an instantaneous hedonic calculus applied to strike a balance between maximizing both our points-per-minute efficiency and the all-important razzamatazz-per-possession quotient. Before that, though, we had to develop a defensive ethos. Hours of experience illuminated the two most effective strategies: decking the guy that inbounded the ball just as his teammate went to pass it back to him, and lighting our players on fire and shamelessly goaltending for halves at a time. With precisely timed pushes, it wasn't unheard of to score dozens of points before the computer brought the ball past half-court. By the time they got that far there would surely be an on-fire defender ready to snatch the ball right off the rim in the event a shot somehow occurred.

We chose the Seattle Supersonics for our endeavor. We were not Supersonics fans. (In fact, as die-hard Bulls fans, we would come to harbor a particular hostility toward the Sonics and one Frank Brickowski in particular. Brickowski was the instigator then-coach George Karl deployed with the intent of getting in Dennis Rodman's head in the 1996 NBA Finals. Indelible in my mind is the image of a frustrated Brickowski hunched over at the perimeter of the lane, surely steaming from another lost battle with Rodman for a rebound; Bad Boy Dennis stood directly beside him, his posture perfect, clasping his hands behind his back as if addressing his commanding officer. He beamed into the near-distance with such a trollish serenity that you thought for a moment a halo might appear over his head. It was Dennis the Menace getting one over on Mr. Wilson and then somehow convincing his mother that the exact opposite had occurred. No wonder he would later seamlessly slide into pro wrestling appearances; he was a worker in every sense of the word.)

Dennis Rodman was still on the San Antonio Spurs in the *Jam* Era, so before the '96 Finals and Brickowski the Sonics of *NBA Jam* held one distinct advantage over our hometown Bulls: they had two great players. This was a 100% increase over the Bulls' *Jam* roster, which had only Scottie Pippen and a mysteriously absent genome of data where Michael Jordan might once have been. To be sure, our unified front against the soulless "CPU" would not have withstood an argument over who gets to be Scottie before every game. Better still, the Sonics of *NBA Jam* had their great players appropriately divided into the two key archetypes of *NBA Jam* characters: Fast Guy and Dunks Guy. There was Gary Payton, The Glove. Payton was the requisite speed and jumpers guy, and with a league-leading STEAL rating, he was one of the few guys in the game with whom swiping the ball from the offense instead of simply flattening the opposing player with a vulgar shove was a successful tactic. He wasn't automatic from 3-point range, nor was he tall enough to reliably goaltend, but feed him a couple easy lay-ups to secure that infinite turbo on top of his impressive SPEED and he could cover the whole court.

Of course, Payton wasn't added to the game's roster until the release of the "Tournament Edition" that also introduced the 1994 Rookies team (notable for *Jam* developers making the per-haps-sociologically-insightful-but-optically-incongruous decision to give Jason Kidd the African-American player model). The holdover from the original *Jam* cabinet was Shawn Kemp, he of the blessed 9 DUNK rating. To play *NBA Jam* as any less accomplished a dunker would be to play Rock Band on mute, to play *Earthbound* without the scratch-and-sniff strategy guide, to play *Duck Hunt* with the standard controller instead of the light gun. Without enough DUNK cred to pull off the glittering infinite-forward-flip superslam—were you really even playing the game? Kemp's impressive push power and dunking ability was enough to earn your loyalty even as the Prince Charles and Phoenix Suns Gorilla cheats beckoned. With Big Shawn, one hearty shove was guaranteed to loose the ball, and from there it was merely a matter of waiting for The Glove to scoop it up and make the assist.

I don't think we ever actually attained perfection during our

championship run despite this murderer's pair of players. That
detail was not important enough to remember despite it ostensi-
bly being our goal. The only time I do recall bothering to rewind
the tape and re-watch anything was when we executed a last
second steal and buzzer-beater to win an embarrassingly tight
game with the CPU. I recall our win-loss record being as pure as
the Puget Sound by way of remembering how important avoid-
ing that loss had been. Still, we remained rigorous throughout
in making sure the tape was in and recording before every play
session. Conor suspects it is still in his parents' basement somewhere, deteriorating like a lesser childhood memory or a civic
culture of basketball fandom. For whatever reason, putting that
tape in and hitting record made our pursuit of perfection im-
print permanently on our analog memories, unlike an untold
number of other days and weeks we spent together. The assumed
persistence of that tape drives the persistence of the memory.

As the NBA has become inextricably linked with that mid-
90s period of American culture, the Sonics have come to represent the parts of that era that can't be revived. That the team
shared a geographic origin with the similarly buried musical
movement that briefly fashioned alt as pop is perhaps not a coincidence. The trappings of the time might see a resurgence, but
one cannot simply bring back the Sonics the way Iman Shump-
ert endeavors to bring back the flat-top. EA Sports tried, sort of:
they put out a "Tournament Edition" of their 2010 installment
of *NBA Jam* in 2011 and featured the Seattle Supersonics—represented by Kemp and Payton—as an unlockable team. It was
a slick product that remained adequately faithful to *Jam*'s me-
chanics and piled enough bonus teams and features on top to
distract from how shallow the original was by today's standards.
Predictably, even playing as the same Sonics didn't meet the im-

possible standard of fun I maybe misremembered. It couldn't have been the same experience anyway: this was a nostalgia exercise *within* a nostalgia exercise, and one warped by the creeping suspicion that it was the Oklahoma City owners who were being compensated for the use of that emerald and gold logo.

The inclusion of those specific arrangements of digital bits does drive the memory, though. Now that they are of the digital age, their configuration is permanently affixed. The team moved in 2008, a full decade after George Karl was fired, but it may as well have never left the prior millennium for all the memories those post-Payton teams made. In that way, the SuperSonics are unique: the other teams in *NBA Jam* portray the franchises of a given time—the Sonics of *NBA Jam* represent the franchise forever.

[BRI]

LOS ANGELES CLIPPERS

I lose more than I win. It is something that is within my blood—that when I was assembled, that when I was plucked from one world and placed in the next, I was deemed as someone who does not come out on top; there is comfort among the failures.

I've never participated on a team that has won much of anything. As a child, all of my basketball teams were the loveable losers—we were in it for the fun of the game, to run around and get our hearts pumping, to experience the game of basketball without consequence.

We all have those moments of glory—no one wants to be the perennial champion; everyone wants to be the underdog who scrapped their way here, that stood on top of the mountain for a day before being shoved back down the hill.

The Los Angeles Clippers are the worst franchise in NBA history; they are perennial losers. The year the game is released, the Clippers made the playoffs for only the second time in their history, winning more games than the Lakers, their glitzed and glamoured crosstown rivals. Danny Manning, the Clippers' power-forward, led the Kansas Jayhawks to a championship despite the Jayhawks having 11 losses going into the tournament.

The game rewards the losers—if a team gets behind by too many points, everything shifts in their favor so that they can catch up. The opponent starts missing shots: sure-fire dunks skyrocket off of the rim, jump shots rattle around before being spit out onto the court. The CPU will begin playing more aggressive: shoving players off the inbound pass, always looking to go for the steal. The game wants every game to be close, to have the drama of a team catching fire, of storming back, of becoming perfect after so much imperfection.

Here is my moment: a game against a well-oiled machine with all flash and coaches' kids running rampant, scoring at will. I was a coaches' kid too—my father teaching us plays named after basketball cities: Boston, Chicago, L.A. We would form lay-up lines, going at the backboard from either side, as if we were ever in a position where we would be sprung ahead of the pack, dribbling as fast as we could towards the basket—that we could plant our opposite foot and spring off of it, kissing the top of the box and banking the shot home.

I wish I could tell you that this happened to me, that the ball took an odd bounce and wound up in my hands, that I dribbled down the court, remembering to gently press the ball in front of me at an angle so I wouldn't trip over my own feet. That I re-membered to slow down as I approached the basket, that I swept towards the left side of the rim and gently laid the ball in as the crowd applauded. That they had never seen me do anything like that before, that they didn't believe it possible. That, in the twist of being blown out, a fire was ignited, that I blacked out, went unconscious, hit every shot I took.

Instead, the best story I can tell is stealing someone else's: that another child on a fast break streaked down the court, my feet caught in wet clay, that I stood my ground, that our bodies crashed into each other, bruised knees, skin rolling back up the arms of our elbows. That they had to stop the game to untangle our bodies, that I was charged with being reckless. That I sat on the bench until the game was over—there were no theatrics, nothing epic, no twenty-point swing. Long after we drove home, long after I hit the showers, I could still feel the heat from my elbow radiating. I imagined how warm it would feel if I could touch the wound without wincing, about how there should've been more to leave out on the court than just skin.

I am sitting in the fifth-worst seat in the Wells Fargo Center, watching the Philadelphia 76ers lose to the Cleveland Cavaliers, telling myself I don't love the Sixers anymore, and doing my best Jeff Hornacek impression. We are through just the first few minutes of the game, have already turned the ball over on three consecutive possessions, are down by six, and my palm keeps involuntarily patting my right cheek.

That is my Jeff Hornacek—an impression I've come to master.

Hornacek suited up in a home jersey in this building for less than two years in the early 1990s, but we remember him for his free-throw

PHILADELPHIA 76ERS

PLAYER 2

[CTO]

shooting tic. At the line, he would pat his right cheek with his right palm three times, the look on his face one of a concerned and sweaty man watching someone ungently clip a puppy's toenails. Woe is Hornacek shooting two.

I am back in the Sixers' arena for the first time in several years, and, from the fifth-worst seat in the house, I can feel Hornacek's spirit.

I am here with my partner—bless her heart—having dragged her to this mid-season nightmare. Almost immediately upon arriving at our royal blue, hard plastic seats in the second-to-last row of the stadium, higher than the lowest rafter, directly behind the visitor's hoop—a vantage point that oblongs the court to a trapezoid and flattens jump shots to their vertical dimension—the lights cut out. A beat. Darkness. A projection, the exact dimensions of the court, is laid over the actual court below it, and lights up the arena.

For a moment it glows there, court over court, in silence.

Then, a crack and the floorboards splinter out from the center's painted logo, as if in the footpath of a colossal invisible something. Another. And another. Great indents made into the hologrammed hardwood. Finally the floor drops off completely, only the painted logo-ring at center court remains. The warble and drop of low-end-heavy electronic music begins, and 3-D projections of dunks and blocks and fists pounding chests appear on the court.

As a non-Sixers fan (which, for your sake, I certainly hope you are) you'd be forgiven for finding this video exciting and novel in its floor-as-jumbotron conceit or for reading the court-destroying in the standard sports-talk of *tearing it up*.

But from the fifth-worst seat, the meaning is clear: we are being trolled.

Ever since we hired the MBA-schooled, silicon-valley reared, advanced-metrics-minded, no-heart-having, dirty rotten Sam Hinkie as our general manager, we have been intentionally losing games. A tactic that is more commonly known as tanking. We've won only five so far this year, none in this arena. Last year we lost 26 in a row.

Lose now to win later—the mindset goes—by racking up the losses, we ensure a higher pick in the next year's draft and theoretically secure a winning future. We've done this for two years now. It's yet to pay off. After his first year, only one player from the pre-Hinkie squad remained. In return, we are suited with picks through the 2019 draft, have a rotation fleshed-out by D-Leaugers on non-guaranteed contracts, and a team salary under the league minimum. We are a team assembled to lose games spectacularly. It's not like we're missing shots on purpose. There's no need. We don't stand a chance of making many in the first place.

Tearing it up, indeed.

Watching the Sixers is an exercise in masochism—an exercise I've regrettably practiced too often this year.

The lights come up, the real court is visible again, the game tips off, and we start our losing. I cast my eyes to my shoes, stuck to the gritty and soda-syruped floor, trying to keep my hands in my lap. I tell myself that I don't love the Sixers anymore.

Though short-lived, Hornacek's tenure in Philly is important for three reasons. One: the aforementioned free-throw attempt tic. Two: He came to Philadelphia by way of the trade that sent Charles Barkley to Phoenix—a top-five worst trade of all time that happened just as I came of Sixers-cheering age. But three, and most important: Jeff Hornacek, the 6'3" shooting guard from Iowa State, the 86th pick in the '86 draft, with a vertical jump measured in centimeters, is a 76er in both the Arcade and Tournament editions of *NBA Jam*.

A few years before Hornacek got pixelated on screens all over the country, I was born into a house in West Philadelphia with three older brothers, a dog named after former Sixers center Moses Malone, and without good cable or videogames. This made the infrequent, brother-chaperoned and -financed trips to Phat City arcade on South Street, a few blocks up from the arena, too crucial.

I didn't know how to drive, the guns on the shooting games never seemed to work at the steep angle us smurfs had to hold them, and there were no baseball games at Phat City. So we walked right past Cruisin' USA and Area 51, and inevitably blew our funds on a single sad and wonderful game of *NBA Jam*.

Sad because if you combine the dunk statistics of Hersey Hawkins and Jeff Hornacek, our roster in that arcade edition, then you've probably got the same combined dunk statistics as you and me. You couldn't pick two more unqualified people in the league to play together in this game. Dunk-wise, Hornacek and Hawkins were the worst, no question. They even played the same position—shooting guard—so they were the worst in the same ways: shooters in a game where, if you've got the slightest vertical inclination, you jump twice as high as the rim. Plus there aren't even any free throws.

The woe is only compounded by the fact that I was no good at video games. I am a button masher, a little brother, a perpetual player two.

But it was also wonderful because *Jam* demanded that I double down on the Sixers. Those games at Phat City were the first bluntly-put questions of allegiance. So, for love of the team,

I still paid quarters by the quarter to look down and make sure I was hitting the right button while getting dispossessed of the ball, or mashing buttons blindly and launching half-court shots. Which, considering our lineup, was actually an okay strategy.

They had to be the most un-fun team to play with. But also then, as a weary Stan of Philly sports who refused to play with any other team, they were technically the *most* fun team to play with, too (pretending to control players on the demo-screen notwithstanding). But its being the worst was also the point. It somehow made us love it more.

Looking back, the double-bound deprecating love makes so much sense. During my childhood, things were starting to pick up in Philly after the industrial decline of the 70s and early 80s, but Fast Eddie was the mayor, the city was insolvent, and everyone was still trying to come to grips with the fact that City Hall had firebombed the MOVE house in West Philadelphia only a few years back.

As kids, while we weren't savvy to the broader frequencies at work, we had a parallel track to teach us the Philadelphia state of mind. It's not Rocky who wins the fight in that first movie and we built the guy a goddamn statue for it. Plus, the nonfiction Phillies got Joe Carter-ed in 93 and only won a game for every Hornacek dunk for the rest of the decade. The Sixers themselves had managed only 35 wins with Barkley, and no matter how hard you mashed on the button, you were never going to get a BOOMSHAKALAKA out of Hawk or Horny.

The *Jam* rosters chronicle the Dark Age of Sixers basketball.

And though Clarence Witherspoon's presence on the SNES Tournament edition got us a player with a dunk stat of 6 (6! I could actually play the game as intended) he didn't really change much on the court. They lost more games each subsequent year from 90-96. And with Barkley and then, ahem, Hornacek, gone, Weatherspoon in *Jam* was really the only spot of brightness in the gloom of that decade. Luckily the neighbors had Nintendo and we spent our allotted 30 minutes savoring the 32-pixelations of Witherspoon dunks.

I know that this is the stuff of garden-variety nostalgia—the chipped-shoulder, love-in-vain, sentimentally self-loathing 90s kid asked to look back on his childhood. But I'm realizing, as these memories find me again in the 5th worst seat in the Wells Fargo arena, that this longing and loving and loathing, in the context of watching the Sixers intentionally lose games, has kudzu-ed itself into a stranger sort of wilderness.

It sometimes feels like it requires a degree in metaphysics to follow the Sixers right now. Is a win a win? A loss a win? A win a loss? In the first- and second-worst seats, directly behind us, are two teenage boys who each hold pails of soda with both hands. Emblazoned on the souvenir cups are images of our rookie center Nerlens Noel in various poses of excellence. On the 2-D trapezoidal court below, he has four points and three fouls. At the bottom of both soda cups is our motto this year: "together we rise."

I tell myself I don't love the Sixers anymore.

You would think that Philadelphia fans would be uniquely equipped to endure a few years of assured losing. We've certainly done it before. I thought that too. But the difference between this losing squad and the '96 losing squad is not a difference of degree, but of kind. All the rest of my friends stopped watching the Sixers last year, content to wait out the tanking and, if it works out, plan to tune in again when we're winning.

I didn't. I couldn't. I started watching more, fascinated and horrified by the cynicism. It's cognitively dissonant in the way that watching Goethe's sorrowful Young Werther give a TED Talk about the benefits of shorting financial markets would be.

Farther uptown from the Wells Fargo and Phat City, off the Ben Franklin Parkway and a stone's throw from the Rocky statue, is the Rodin museum. It's a modest building, tucked between the Free Library and the Art Museum. It's got a collection of casts from French sculptor Auguste Rodin, from the very Hornacekian *The Thinker* to the first bronze casting of *The Gates of Hell*. "For Rodin," the catalogue notes, "the chaotic population on *The Gates of Hell* enjoyed only one final freedom—the ability to express their agony with complete abandon."

I spent the afternoon of my last pre-Hinkie birthday walking with my parents through the garden of the Rodin museum. The place was being revamped but still open and in front of Rodin's masterpiece we found this sign: "We apologize for our appearance while *The Gates of Hell* undergoes renovation."

I was broke in more ways than one that summer, living with my parents back in Pennsylvania as I tried to get un-broke, and I cannot tell you the deep joy I took in finding that sign hanging in the main concourse of the city in which I was born. It was like they had set it out for me.

That sign captured both the problem with, and solution to, the Philadelphia state of mind. That the acknowledgment of one's despair, done with enough frankness and sadness and humor and irony can actually become a refutation of that very same despair—calling for Adrian at the end of the lost fight. That, if you do it right, its not a void into which you howl, but a city, a team, a sense of self.

Whether it was Stockholm syndrome or some deeply-rooted need to feel okay about myself again by feeling okay about my childhood obsession, that sign made me fall in love with Philadelphia all over again.

Not that I'm in love with defeat, but with the idea that every project should admit its own futility without collapsing the whole endeavor. To come back home and have it feel new. To commit to honestly loving another while still struggling to know yourself. To know the impossibility of language to fully render experience, but to still write. To begin an essay eddying around ideas without a clear path in mind. In short, in the nonfiction writer's eponymous credo: to assay, to attempt.

At the start of the crack up that brought me to the Rodin garden, I read Fitzgerald's ode to the condition over and over again, as I bussed through the midwest flatness back to Pennsylvania. "One should, for example, be able to see that things are hopeless" Fitzgerald writes "and yet be determined to make them otherwise."

I chose the team. I chose them even though this goddamn double bind might very well have contributed to my hobble, it would now be my crutch. I decided I could love myself in the way I first learned to love: for better and for worse.

Forgive me if this sounds hopelessly sincere and sentimental, but part of recommitting to the mindset of Philly sports was done under the assumption that this was a space away from the crippling cynicism and more enervating aspects of this modern life. That I wouldn't have to offer a corrective, in essay form, about the foundational sincerity on which sports are predicated.

But just as I re-immersed myself in the orders and patterns of basketball and consented to mental health treatment for the first time, we started tanking. And we did it without the goddamn decency to put a sign in front of the Wells Fargo Center that begs our pardon for their appearance.

The heartache has become too acute. I tell myself that I don't, I can't love the Sixers anymore.

I'm reminded, in that fifth-worst seat, while looking at the retired numbers of Sixers players, that the teams of my youth were not all woe. There's a new number hanging in the rafters since the last time I've been to a Sixers game. Last year, at the exact midpoint of our record-tying 26 game losing streak, the team retired Allen Iverson's number.

Allen Iverson, 5'11" with heel inserts, singlehandedly did what a decade's worth of Sixers players tried and failed to do: he won games. Often singlehandedly.

Iverson's zenith in Philly came in 2001: a 56-26 record while cinching the scoring title, All-Star MVP, and league MVP.

He was a spectacular underdog, on the verge of realizing all the city's dreams in exactly the way we dreamed them. I remember a graphic from that year's playoffs, detailing the injuries sustained across Iverson's whole body from sprained toe to neck stingers, some of which undoubtedly coming from the weight of carrying the entire franchise on his back. Yet he started every game and consistently put up 30+ points (only Jordan has a better career playoff scoring average). Three of those points coming when, in the finals that year he crossed over Tyronn Lue so bad he fell to the court, hit the three, and then stepped over Lue still on the floor in front of the Laker bench, before trotting back on D. But we couldn't escape our destiny. We lost the next four games. We haven't been back to the Finals since.

And though Iverson was nothing if not paradoxical—the love-hate relationship with coach Larry Brown, the scoring titles won on 28 shot attempts per game, the most beloved Philly player who never won a ring—it's impossible to square him with the paradoxes of tanking. The fans, and to some degree the city, are still under the hold of Iverson's ethos. He embodies the attempt in vain better than any Philadelphian, whereas tanking makes the trying redundant. The futility is now in fandom.

That's why tanking now to win later hurts so bad: because it won't matter.

Like the body replacing all its cells every seven years—the players, the coaches, the owners, the GM—the Sixers are all new and all business. If the process the management takes to get us to a championship indicates to us in no uncertain terms that fans and players and people generally don't matter, why care if a conglomerate of mercenaries with high player efficiency ratings get a ring? The messy human loss is more resonant here than the sterilized, Fitbit-fueled win. The statistically-driven *NBA Jam* might appeal to Hinkie's nature, but that dude could never write an essay.

But, last month, when we were 0-17, headed for the worst start in the history of the league, our point guard Michael Carter Williams was driven to assay, publishing a personal piece in the *Player's Tribune* titled "Don't Talk to Me About Tanking."

He's no longer on the roster.

Only breaking your heart can make you love. Maybe that's the rub: that tanking obviates that basic human part of sports. Intentionally losing now to chase some certainty of winning down the road is heartless and just plain boring. Ethical ideals and TV ratings aside, it gets at the reason for watching sports: the vulnerability evoked by loving a team who might lose.

If the arcade was still standing, I'd wager a day's worth of *NBA Jam* games at Phat City that the '01 Finals loss will matter more than a Hinkie-guided championship in 2019.

I tell myself I don't love the Sixers anymore.

Though I know this to be true—that this season was done before it started—here I am somehow, on my feet, cheering for this godforsaken group of players who have somehow closed the 12-point gap in the fourth quarter, and, on a beautiful drive with eight seconds remaining, Tony Wroten, who can't even dribble with his left hand, crosses Dion Waters over and hits the game winning shot. We have won. A sloppy game against the Cleveland bench in a meaningless season. But we had won.

My hand goes to my cheek.

Long after the game, we linger in the upper deck. The victory song has played and most of the crowd has filed out, but still we stay. I pat my cheek again.

Earlier that night, the Phoenix Suns, now coached by Hornacek, beat the upstart Toronto Raptors by 20 points. The Suns hired Hornacek last year, planning to tank. Instead, he got them winning, barely missing the playoffs in a crowded Western Conference. Hornacek was second in Coach of the Year voting.

The attempt is what matters.

The kids behind us in the first- and second-worst seats in the stadium are gone. They left as soon as the buzzer hit, looking at their phones, leaving their commemorative soda pails in front of their seats. I pat my cheek again, worrying and hoping that they've been spared the fate of loving this team. The last two in the stands, my partner and I make our way down the steps, but I double back and grab both their cups. Just to have. Just in case.

[BRI]

HOUSTON ROCKETS

There is an inherent need to let the world know that we were here, that we existed at a time and a place beyond the moment that we are currently in. There needs to be a cohabitation of worlds in order for there to even be one world: where we are now is a result of a combination of layers that have existed forever. We leave our marks in every way possible: through recipes passed down and kept secret from people who do not share our bloodlines, through sculptures on bookshelves that once belonged to hands well before ours, through children. The first thing that the game asks you to do is to make your mark: to enter your initials for record-keeping—to make sure that not only when you return to the game you can pick up where you left off, but if you do something extraordinary, it can let the world know, or, at the very least, the sons and daughters who begged their parents for a quarter while the pizza was still being cut into eighths and put into boxes.

My initials are BO. My mother apologized for this when I was older: said she had loved the name *Brian*, that it was written in the stars, that she had thought about how it could possibly be dooming me to a life of body odor jokes, and extra long showers, and thousands of dollars I do not have spent on covering up with fragrances with heavy base notes.

There have been studies that say children with positive initials live longer: that something in the runes alludes to the fact that they were coded better—ACE, WIN, VIP, DNA, RNA. Those with negative names—PIG, ASS, DIE—die almost three years earlier than normal. For some reason, accidents find them, that the reaper whispers in their ears more often.

My signature always includes an E: a big sloppy lightning bolt of a thing, a shaky claw, a way to break up what has trailed me since birth. When I am asked to initial something, I always squeeze an extra letter in the small space; I acknowledge and accept these terms.

We talk about the Rockets with a caveat: that they excelled in the absence of greatness, that they took advantage of a time in which all of the cheat codes were disabled, that this was the simulation of the game at its worst. When the game was originally being developed, the programmers promised that it would be the most realistic game on the market, that there would be no razzle-dazzle, no giant heads, no moments of superhumanity transcending what occurs behind closed doors in high school gymnasiums.

The game is not a circus. There was no way to make you remember this: that you don't remember putting in your own name, you don't remember where it asked for the date of your birth. Most days, we gave up ourselves to be someone else: there were rumors of the game allowing you to become something larger than even a basketball player—you could be president. You could be anyone beside yourself—the son of a programmer, a cheerleader. You could unlock Jordan. You could become death.

I have a fear of vastness: of deep water, of sprawling landscapes. My greatest fear is of space, of how the universe expands infinitely—that there is a chance that a small push with zero gravity can send me spiraling into the unknown, doubling over and over until I disappear—the oxygen depletes, the lights go out, and my body drifts forever. I do not understand how rockets work, how we send humans up and over the atmosphere, how we haven't found anything out there that hasn't float away.

When the game asks me to keep a record, I reply with BRI instead of BO or BEO: a shortening of a name, an insinuation that I could be any BRIAN that has ever existed—that I have renounced my father's EDWARD, that I have renounced my grandfather's OLIU, that I am cursory, that I am selfish, that I am simultaneously here and not here, that all I am is an avatar of letters, that I have spent my life in the glyphs of someone else.

This is the beginning of the artifice: that before I even embody anyone, I must pull a ghost from my own mouth to speak for me even though my voice goes silent in the void. This is all pretend. This is already more than I bargained for.

[BRI]

ORLANDO MAGIC

There is a room for freaks in basketball, but not too many. We cannot disturb the status quo. They must be sideshows, reasons to bring your family, to put popcorn in the hands of as many on-lookers as possible.

This was never a game for someone like me—flat-footed, slow-footed, every pivot a lumbering. The jerseys wouldn't fit over my body: they should be big enough for someone my age, they would say, and it was true—I was an anomaly, a statue of clumsy. I would wear the shirt meant for the coaches—a man's shirt, despite being nothing but: someone who couldn't do anything except sit in front of televisions, one hand on the controller and the other one sticky from chocolate that had melted between the grooves of my fingerprints.

I hated Shaquille O'Neal: I hated how large he was, how everyone in suburban New Jersey loved him despite his size, how easily allegiances shifted. I hated how easy this game was for him, how someone that large can make the world bend to his will, how he had the luxury to operate within a different set of rules while I was being kicked in the stomach—that I couldn't feel pain beyond the layers of fat.

Shaq would disappear in later iterations of the game, his likeness becoming too large for the game of basketball, his multitudes sprawling out in gushes. O'Neal negotiated a deal separate from the one made between the player's union and the association, and thus the price tag was too expensive to include him in the game. The audacity of this—to believe that basketball was simply one thing that he can do in this world, that there is still so much of him to be put toward filming movies, recording albums.

I read an article about him when I was younger; about how when he was a child he would slouch, about how all he wanted to be was normal. I shared this too: there is no virtue in being someone that everyone else is not.

A memory: a school field trip to a museum of the body. At the center of the museum, a large-scale version of the human heart that children could walk through—they could touch the insides of ventricles, could spin around in an atrium. There are vessels too—small tubes that children can crawl through, pretend to be something smaller than what they are, be parts of an amazing whole. As I crouched to fit, a woman grabbed my arm, told me that I was too large to fit, that I could get stuck. I stood next to models of other hearts, of animals larger and smaller than I was. They spiraled toward the sky. There must be a way to take my heart out from underneath all of this virtue and muscle and see where it belongs—in a world where I am the largest bird, but the smallest ape, there is nothing but extremes to discuss. I have always been disappointed in the scale of things, of percentiles, of *where I stand*s.

Another field trip: one of medical oddities. It is where I will go when I die. They will put me in a glass case, they will have my skull on the ground where children can open up the bottom of my jaw. The children will make me talk, make me say things I never could when I was alive. There will be a body next to mine; it will be O'Neal's. They will be amazed that he is here, that this museum could afford such a priceless artifact, that it should be elsewhere, draped in gold, in a vault somewhere, hooked up to a machine that makes the man animatronic—telling wide-eyed jokes with a flashing nose. Instead, children will stand inside of our bodies; they will imagine what it would've been like to live this large—to be this small inside. I will finally understand. I will finally contain multitudes. I will not move from this place.

THE SOUTH GOT SOMETHING TO SAY
North and South. We always come
in second. We always want people
to notice us fight. We know we won't
win. We're a region of Hectors tired
of running from God's plan. We're
only a shadow, an echo. Harvard of
the South. Pittsburgh of the South.
Jay Z of the South. We're regional.
You didn't make it out of Georgia until jumping to scrape heaven melted
your knees. I could call you Icarus,
call you a fool for trying to keep up
with Boston and Chicago. Didn't they
ever tell you how slow Southern boys
were supposed to be? Nobody told
you that you were supposed to put
up a good fight and hang your head

ATLANTA HAWKS

PLAYER 2

[M R J]

when another man waved his banner over your home? Nobody told you that we would sell you off and make you watch your city burn like Priam's daughters. You were supposed to be another trophy on a better man's wall. You weren't supposed to beat him in the 1985 Slam Dunk Contest. It wasn't in Spike Lee's script. The Jumpman logo doesn't show you jumping higher than him. I was born in 1984, but I love 1985 because Vince McMahon made *Wrestlemania* and you beat an unbeatable man.

All I ever wanted in life was a man who could beat Him. I won't say His name because, like a true god or ghoul, we can't say His name here. But you know Him. I spent summers digging through averages. Look, this player was a better foul shooter. Look, this guy had twice as many steals. I found a champion when Starks went baseline. I fell for the Drexler comparison. I laced up my Kamikazes and hoped. When Iverson crossed Him over, I stopped caring about any of the court cases. But, for six Junes, I played Priam while I watched each new champion fall and pay tribute. The world paid tribute. Every shaved head. Every kid killing himself trying to dunk in a backyard. Every rec league air reverse. Every *pang* of a cheap basketball against the concrete. Every fight in a Foot Locker line.

Damn, I'm doing it, too, Dominque. I'm making you a footnote. This should be about you and how you should have been on the Dream Team and how Atlanta just can't stop selling black bodies. When I learned about you beating Him one time, I heard Andre 3000 at the Source awards. I wasn't there, but that never stopped a Southerner from claiming a story as his own. I didn't see it, but I can see it. I know what it must have looked like.

PLASTIC MAN

"Plastic Man with a Plastic Man Jam!" I still think about your name whenever a wiry body slices to the basket. I had to you; you have a superhero name. I'll rep for Superman first, but Batman said you kill us all. But I don't want you to kill anyone; I want you to kill a dream, all the dreams coated in panted leather and wagging tongues. *Space Jam* gave up the secret. Every one of your dunks was like the last scene of the movie. Arm stretched to an impossible length. The hopeless arms of defenders reaching for a heaven they'll never know. I just needed a hero who could stretch an inch farther than He can. How many Gatorade commercials would die if Ehlo had your arms? How many of those Portland three-pointers could you have challenged with your impossible arms? You were the prototype. If I had to design a player to beat Him, it might have been you. The bald head. A goatee to let the world know about your rebel edge. In a dumb boy's eyes, you could almost pass for Him. Just as quick. Taller. Rangier. Younger. But even with those long arms, the ball never seemed to reach the basketball enough. For every dunk, there was the clang of the rim in unison with the shot clock's death note. The arms stretched one second too late. The arms could reach to the moon, but they couldn't point out a pick. You weren't made of plastic; you couldn't reach any farther than a few put-back dunks and lefty jumpers. And lefty jumpers only go so far, even with me. You weren't Plastic Man; you were just a man. You weren't a hero, but you weren't everything you could be, either. I saw you do so much in a video game. Do you know how many steals you had when your arms were my arms? Do you know how many basketballs you clawed out of the sky like a wolf swallowing the sun when I was there to tell you the ball won't burn your hands? I know it's in you. I know you've been programmed to be better than this. Be a hero. Do it for Batman. Do it for the world.

[BRI]

PHILADELPHIA 76ERS

There is an ownership when playing video games—you are simultaneously outside of the game, but also within. When we die when gaming, we claim the deaths as our own: we do not often say that our character has died; instead, we say that we have died: *I've* been hit, or *I* fell in the lava.

This is where I stood: top of the key, towering above the world like a scaffold whose building has long since been erected. The game happened around me while I was standing still. The ball would be passed around the perimeter, but never towards the middle. The slick kids would take the ball in the backcourt and dribble into a corner—away from defenders until boxed in. This is something that I knew would happen, but was powerless to do anything about. I would tell myself to focus— that this would be the best game I'd ever played, that I would take over, that I could become all things, that nothing would ever be the same, that all calls for the ball would not echo off the pushed in bleachers, that this would all mean something more than an exercise in what the body is capable of witnessing.

I was never one to run the court quickly. I was always the last to get in position on offense. I would give up faster than the other children solely because it took me longer to get back on defense. I would look for bad shots and turn and run, knowing that there is no foot races that I can win handily. I never shot the ball except when it was absolutely necessary: when the ball would bounce into my hands, arms immediately go up, eyes locked onto mine, calling for the ball, all voices ready to shame me if I dared to take a single dribble.

To win at the game, you have to do the heavy lifting: you have a teammate who will run the court—they will always inbound the ball to you—they will never look for the shot. You can tell them when to shoot; when to pass the ball. Other games are not like this: most sports games allow you to embody as many players as you wish, your ghost-like presence indicated with a green arrow floating above their heads. Here, it lets you know where you stand: your initials tagged to your body, outsiders with the letters *CPU* floating in front of theirs.

The majority of the game is beyond your control. You can choose which team you want to play as. You can select which of the two players you want to possess. Beyond that, there is nothing but variables: shots that seem like they should go in without a problem clang off the back of the rim. Opponents grab miracle rebounds. Your teammate gets shoved to the ground without shoving back.

There is precedent in *creating one's shot* in basketball—the ability to drive past a defender to an open space without the help of your teammates to rise above the person in front of you and shoot over them, to reduce the game to one-on-one. The strategy in the game is to take the ball off the inbound and run to the other end of the court as fast as possible in order to beat your defender back—to score as many points as possible in a short amount of time, as the game will always battle back.

The Sixers, as we know them here, are never for the choosing. They are perennial opponents, only being chosen by Player 1 out of loyalty for a franchise, a father living just outside of Philadelphia, a love for the glory years of Moses and Irving, Chamberlain and Greer. Here, journeymen, trade pieces to make larger deals work, good shooters when left alone in space, when found by a driving force for a kick-out three in the corner.

At some point, players must look at themselves and ask what they must do in order to stay in the game: after a torn left calf muscle, after the cartilage is erased from years of jumping—bone grinding against bone with every step. Jeff Hornacek is the head coach of the Suns now. Hersey Hawkins is the director of player development for the Trail Blazers. How lucky I must have been to have my knees intact, my body not broken with the exception of a few fingers that bend inward. This is not a lesson that I ever needed to learn; there's no need to hang it up if there is nothing to hang—all the hooks rusted and dangling.

I'd like to tell you that I was born to coach this game, that I had a keen eye for running in space despite standing still like a monolith, that I could guide men stronger than I am away from the flood. Despite all of this, basketball is a game that happens in the moments where it happens; it is too quick for anything else. Coaching occurs when the game does not: over summers in hot gyms, when the clock is stopped. I told you I've never had enough power for this; I could never dictate the world. The game never slowed down for me. I've never seen a bounce pass come to me in slow motion, never felt the power spring from my calves to my wrist. The only control that I have is the knowledge that things are beyond my control, yet I'm still too stubborn to not believe in anything.

[BRI]

SACRAMENTO KINGS

Basketball is a game about angles, about the shortest path from one spot on the floor to another, about how the ball bounces off the rim, about where your feet should be set. In the game, when the players get closer, they get larger—they double in size to the point where you can see their features: a face becomes a face rather than a collection of pixels, eyes straight forward and never blinking. This is forced perspective: an adjustment of scale in relation to what the eye sees, the making of things brighter so that the court blurs in the background. It is all an illusion: despite getting closer, we do not grow in size—we simply are what we are despite what our wavering eyes are trying to tell us.

When I grew older, I went to Italy: I saw a church where the ceiling was flat, but painted to look like there was a dome—a *trompe l'oeil*, a trick of the senses. The legend was that the church next door petitioned to the city that the construction would block out their sunlight, that the skyline was already too crowded with monoliths. Instead, a painting where the goal was to make the viewer believe that there was more nothing than what appeared. We stared for what seemed like forever: our heads cocked back, chins towards the sky. While the story of the church in Rome is that the new ceiling would crowd the air, the truth is that it was cheaper to paint a ceiling than to extend it upwards. We spun in the middle of baroques, we tried to find the angle that made the whole thing less real: we cannot be impressed by something if we believe it to be entirely true—then, a nave is just a nave and not what it is pretending to be.

We remember Spud Webb as being the smallest person we've ever seen, though he was only two inches shorter than average: a man who could look most folks in the eye without much effort. We remember his leaps in the Slam Dunk contest—how we marveled at how someone that small could get that high—that everything he did seemed grand in comparison to someone who could touch the rim without their feet off of the ground.

When Wayman Tisdale went in for cancer treatments, the doctor said they'd never given chemotherapy to anyone his size. When they amputated Wayman Tisdale's leg, they created the largest prosthesis the doctor had ever seen. When you play the game you notice this: how large the man is—how tall he stretches in comparison.

I never took a photo with my hands holding up the Tower of Pisa. I never wanted it to look like I had the ability to do so, that

I was so large I could make buildings tip over, that the second I held my hands to the air in the forefront, the earth would move and the tower would fall.

So, when I tell you that I was the biggest kid you've ever seen, that is an illusion, something parents would scream when I stood next to their child, that I dwarfed their baby, that I am too dangerous to be allowed to play, that I should be with children my own size, despite them being much older. That my elbows could too easily catch a nose, that I was an oaf in an oaf's body, that everything was unfair. I was never here to hurt anyone. I was never here to make your children bleed. There is a reason why big kids have soft hearts—one false move and our size will be blamed for everything; the game will be over, the rules will be changed. There is a reason I played basketball—it made it more difficult to hurt someone: no cleats to the face, no shoulders to the sternum. If you fight me, I will hurt you. I am a warning. If I hurt you, we were just playing. I took everything too far; I threw my weight around; I missed my mark. The term *monster* will always be relative—there is always someone larger. There is always someone more hideous.

Here is what I prayed: that the world would catch up, that nature could shift, that the order of things brought a demonstration to every doorstep. I would stay awake, not asking for the world to make me smaller, but for the world to get bigger: the curse of a slowed metabolism, the shame of a fat child. I was not put here to be a king: to die after having trouble breathing—of trying to fill a space with air yet having the walls remain flat. Put me in a world of giants. Let them marvel at how I fill the cracks in the design.

There's a glitch in *NBA Jam* only John Starks knows about. He sits in the dark in his duplex, the gummy carpet littered with empty forties and dead blunts. He selects his old squad, the New York Knicks, and chooses himself as the playable character. He looks at his face onscreen—grinning fifty years earlier—and taps in the code. In the twilight of his life, John Starks has discovered how to summon Michael Jordan in *NBA Jam*.

Jordan refused to lend his likeness to the *NBA Jam* developers because he signed his own, more lucrative deal to star exclusively in *Michael Jordan: Chaos in the Windy City*, an unplayable 16-bit debacle almost on

NEW YORK KNICKS

PLAYER 2

[SAL]

par with Shaquille O'Neal's video game holocaust *Shaq-Fu*. But John Starks doesn't know any of this. All John Starks knows is the code came to him in the middle of the night during one of his sleep terrors. He saw it neon red, pulsating on his ceiling. Up seventeen times. *Then the* B *button. Unlock Michael Jordan in* NBA Jam. That was three weeks ago. John Starks hasn't left home since.

The game boots up and Horace Grant wins the tip. He kicks the ball to Michael Jordan, who leaps from the three-point line and dunks the ball. John Starks grinds his teeth as the announcer shouts, "Razzle dazzle!" The game is glitched. John Starks has to believe the game is glitched. In *NBA Jam*, Michael Jordan is faster than everyone, stronger than everyone. He can shoot without missing from anywhere on the floor. Three weeks of playing and John Starks has yet to even score a basket against Michael Jordan and his cackling sidekick Horace Grant. Starks's partner, Patrick Ewing, crouches under the basket and weeps. When he finally inbounds the ball, Jordan steals it from digital John Starks and dunks it so hard the hoop explodes. Glass rains down on digital John Starks as the announcer screams, "Hoop's on fire! Hoop's on fire!"

John Starks closes his eyes and tries to ignore the announcer's cries, the fire and brimstone on his dinky television set. As a boy he felt certain he would end up in hell, but he would have never imagined it coming for him through the decayed visage of his son's Super Nintendo. The greatest professional moment of John Starks's life occurred during a 1993 playoff game against the Bulls. With less than a minute to go in the fourth quarter, his small frame elevated skyward and he tomahawk-jammed in the faces of the much taller Horace Grant and Michael Jordan. But the Knicks lost the series. They lost out to the Bulls four times in the playoffs during Starks's tenure. For the last fifty years he's had to endure old fans telling him that if it weren't for Jordan, the '90s Knicks would have been the greatest dynasty in the history of sports. John Starks opens his eyes and watches Michael Jordan urinate all over digital John Starks's face. Patrick Ewing is bleeding out in the background, his intestines balled in his hands. Michael Jordan rips out digital John Starks's heart and raises it above his head like a sacrament.

John Starks stands up for the first time in three weeks. He is eighty years old and doesn't know how he's still alive. He puts on his raincoat and braves the short distance outside to his Buick. He listens to the engine rev and imagines tying Jordan to a chair and dunking over his body until the end of time. All debts have to be settled.

John Starks arrives at Michael Jordan's mansion three hours later. He's shocked to discover it in disrepair. The iron gate at the property's edge is toppled, eaten inside out by rust. The road that leads to the mansion is pockmarked with potholes, the grass alongside it running leafy and wild in all directions. He parks in front of the entrance, the wooden doors lifeless on the ground, and tilts his head skyward. John Starks is here.

It's dark inside, so John Starks retrieves a lighter from his coat pocket and strikes a flame. He makes out a foyer, the furniture sealed in plastic, a thick coat of dust over everything. He hears windows clanging against the mansion and the faint whistle of wind. He comes to a marble staircase and follows it up to a hallway at the end of which John Starks spots a red oak door nearly as big as his Buick. He hesitates before opening it, terrified that the pixilated Michael Jordan of NBA Jam might leap out at any moment to tear out his heart. He slips inside and sees a bed and velvet comforter, the rising and falling body of a man sleeping beneath it. John Starks creeps forward quietly, oh so quietly, and reaches the head of the bed. He recognizes the old man's face under a powder blue nightcap: Michael Jordan.

He stands there unsure of what to do. He never really had a plan, just vague ideas of malice and retribution. But now that he's here, now that Michael Jordan's face is really before him, John Starks is indecisive. Does he really want to kill Michael Jordan? Was it really Michael Jordan's fault that John Starks injured his knee the year MJ hammed it up in AA baseball? Was it Michael Jordan's fault that John Starks was traded from the Knicks in 1999, that his career never recovered? Was it Michael Jordan's fault that John Starks even had to play four humiliating games as a Bull in 2000, long after MJ retired with his six championship rings? Was it Michael Jordan's fault that John Starks lost touch with his son during that decade squandered to the trenches of the NBA? Was it Michael Jordan's fault that everyone had to die someday? John Starks stands there, stands there some more. Finally he tugs back the comforter and gets into bed with Michael Jordan. He hugs the old bastard and MJ blinks his eyes open. He whispers, "John Starks? Is that you?" and John Starks tells him it is.

"John Starks." Michael Jordan stretches the words out into four syllables, an incantation. "Do you wish you were a better person?"

"Yes."

"Me too. I was a terrible person."

They hold each other under the velvet comforter. After a few minutes, Jordan falls back to sleep and John Starks listens to his old foe snore. There's something comforting about it, how very human it sounds. It puts Starks at ease, reminds him of whistling, of his grandfather in Tulsa, cupping his neck in his palm and steering John inside the family barbershop. The bell above the barbershop door chimes as John's uncle waves with a pair of scissors. He gives a little boy a baldy sour and the kid smiles at John, his front two teeth missing. His grandfather squeezes John's neck, his fingers warm and sure, radiating love. It could go on forever like this. It could go on forever.

[BRI]

DENVER NUGGETS

The thing about play is that it does not have a language: we learn the rules of a game through action instead of language. The game renders aural learning obsolete; we must watch players make cuts in the lane, we must feel the tackiness of the leather composite on our fingertips.

Basketball has a language, though: we must learn to speak it before we can understand—that there is a beauty in how the ball comes off the backboard, but if we do not use the terminology—*banked in, box and one, swing man*—there is uncertainty in what occurred. We need this validation to keep us whole. When Dikembe Mutombo came to the United States from the Republic of the Congo, he wanted to be a doctor, to help others back home. Instead, he was recruited to play basketball, earning a degree in linguistics—the art of dissecting language to the point of meaning.

I spent a summer in the Pyrenees when I was in middle school. We stayed in the house that my grandfather grew up in outside of Barcelona. There was little to do there for a nine-year-old: I would go swimming in my aunt's pool, the only one for miles. I did not understand the people around me: my grandparents spoke Catalan, German, Spanish, French, but they also spoke English—that even when they were using their tongues to make these noises they could revert back to the language of my youth in order to tell me that dinner was ready, that they loved me, that they wanted me to turn the channel on the television.

There was a boy my age who lived nearby—we would play together, despite each not knowing what the other was saying. We would play soccer until I grew tired: he was much better than I was, and so I wanted to change games to a language that I was more familiar with—that in a world in which I knew nothing, I could teach someone something, that I could be the expert.

There were courts if you walked down towards the valley—past the church where my grandfather was baptized, a short walk into an area where the mountains plateaued. There was a single hoop that shared space with a tennis court: the waist-high net stretched across the middle, the service line splitting the court into thirds. I bought a tennis ball at the shop down the road and I would play—my hands too big to shoot properly, the ball too rubbery to get a proper bounce off the rim, sending it scattering every which way but through the hoop.

The game makes you collaborate with others: a player moving in patterns down the court, passing and shooting when you suggest it with a press of a button. Basketball, like remembering, is lonely. You are responsible for your own actions. We shoot baskets in our driveway by ourselves, we spend nights alone trying to conjure worlds we used to live in, faces we took for granted.

I don't know whatever happened to the boy in the village where my grandfather grew up. I like to imagine he went on to basketball greatness because of our bastardized half-court tennis ball game, much like Mutombo—learning English through the game, learning the game through being on the court. I know what happened to me, though. I find myself on nights trying to translate the words of my grandfather—to write what he wrote in a language that I could understand. I find myself failing, over, and over to comprehend: accent marks that slope and swirl in places that I could never imagine. I am here, collaborating with ghosts—players that dash in zig-zags up and down the court, opportunities and messages lost along the way; the shift of everything thought to be known and known to be loved dissolving on an awkward tongue.

[BRI]

LOS ANGELES LAKERS

I have never seen myself play basketball. I was not good enough to be studied on film, to track my movements, to see which way I would roll (the left, always), how I created my shots. Seeing my body on film is a harrowing experience—it would be even more so to watch me do something that I am not good at. We hope that the world is only interested in documenting our strengths, but there is a love of error—of air balls and blocked shots.

When I am shooting baskets by myself, this is the best basketball player I can possibly be. There are no defenders looking to swipe the ball away; there is no shot clock, no audience, no outside pressures causing me to miss. Every shot is an open shot, which makes every miss even more frustrating— this game will never be any easier. Yet there is loveliness in the quietness. The only thing heard is the echo of the rubber as it bounces off the floor in varying cadences.

The Lakers in the game are in disarray—it is hard to believe that there was a time when a storied franchise was in a rough patch, but here we bear witness: the Showtime Lakers of the 70s and 80s have dissolved with the sudden retirement of Magic Johnson. Gone is the razzle dazzle—the up-tempo fast break. What we are left with is James Worthy at the end of his career and Vlade Divac, both stiff-legged and matte—no slickness, all of the sleekness rubbed away.

The crowd does not change in the game. It is the same collection of sprites in the background. There is a man in a dark suit who repeats himself—an obvious way to cut down on art production. There is no reason to watch the crowd in the game. The action on the court is too fast to pay much attention to the background layers. They cheer when there is a dunk, large sections standing up for a moment before sitting back down while the basketball is brought up into the frontcourt. They boo when someone is shoved to the ground or loses the ball, showing their disdain for ugliness. They have no loyalty to either side; they are there to be entertained, to love the big play, the fast break, the cinematography of it all.

A sportswriter famously said of the L.A. Forum, "You go to The Fabulous Forum, and you get a basketball game in between lounge acts." Basketball is meant to be entertaining: there are flourishes, exclamation points, risings and firings. You buy the game for the dunking, the ability to do flips in the air that could never be imagined—to leave from the free-throw line and spin like a figure skater, to deliver the ball with a satisfying *chunk*. There is nothing majestic about bodies breaking down, the willing of a basket, of fundamentals—chest passes and tight defense; every layup an insult to the audience. There is no one who wishes to witness what it is that I do—no four act play, no ticket stubs taken at the door and held onto, wedged in between the corners of mirrors to remind you of what you have seen.

Where I shoot baskets, there is an indoor track that is suspended above the court—sometimes I see someone I know, headphones on, eyes forward and running. They are doing the same thing I am. Running will never be as easy as these conditions allow: a constant battle between a man and himself to improve. When they see me, they wave and I wave back. I am self-conscious of my shot selection, my follow through. How long have they been watching? How long have I had an audience? I move my feet closer to the basket: I dribble more, take more time in between shots. I stop attempting three-pointers. I put an end to the turn-around jumpers, the hook shots, the runners in the lane. There is nothing fashionable here anymore, nothing to record. I am the lounge act in between greatness. Watch me croon for a laugh before we return to our scheduled programming. When it is all over, no one will save the recording for safekeeping.

The name always made sense to me. Think: David Blaine submerged in an aquasphere for one week. Think: David Copperfield twisting unscathed at the center of a funnel of fire. Or, rather, the thinking comes after the fact. Magic is an effect beyond thought, a brain held in suspension. It's only when you think back on it that you *think* you know what really happened beyond immediate sensation.

The first and only time I visited the Magic Kingdom, I was taken with how outsized everything was. Round lines and large eyes of cartoon figures in every direction. Every building was more grand, more jungle, more pirate, more itself than any other in the

ORLANDO MAGIC

PLAYER 2

[BEG]

world. I adored Epcot—the 'round-the-globe trip through some of the world's major cultures. I wasn't experiencing Japan; I was experiencing an exaggerated, dialed-up Japan. Looking back as an adult I see lots of stereotypes, but through the eyes of a younger self I saw what travel is always supposed to be but rarely is: the world rendered larger than your capacity to understand. Everything, to use the cliché, larger than life.

I suppose what attracted me to the Orlando Magic was their size. I had to have a good reason to root for any specific NBA franchise because Kansas City didn't have a team; the Kings moved to Sacramento the year before I was born. Chicago was closest to me but this was the era of Jordan. Deciding to be a Bulls fan would've been cheating. I don't remember if I knew how bad the Orlando Magic had been, but it was that streak of poor play that landed the team Shaquille O'Neal and Anfernee "Penny" Hardaway. Shaq was comic-book-villain-big, like the Juggernaut, plowing down the court. His power broke backboards. He might have had his own gravitational field that pulled passes out of orbit and into his palms. I remember reading a story in *Sports Illustrated for Kids* on Shaq's size 22 wide shoes. There was a picture of his shoe against his head like a telephone and I thought that it had to be a trick. Nothing could be that big. But it wasn't so much Shaq that got me to follow the Magic as it was Penny Hardaway, a gifted athlete at an unusually-tall-for-the-point-guard-position 6'7". He was a blur of lanky limbs hurtling towards the basket, tossing up-and-unders from the Dr. J spot, or jamming the ball with force from the baseline, or throwing no-look passes back to Shaq off the dribble-drive. Every moment seemed bigger with those two in it.

> "I put a spell on you/and now you're mine."
> —Bette Midler, *Hocus Pocus* (1993)

My love for *NBA Jam* did not come from a place of hero worship. I did not need to see these players pull off full-court threes or 540° somersault dunks; Penny & Shaq were already of cartoon proportions, were already redefining human possibility for me. Instead I loved *NBA Jam* because of hero *aspiration*. I didn't care if Horace Grant, playing against type, drained a flaming ball from the top of the key. I cared that *I* did it. I cared that I was at the controls, responsible in some small way for an athletic accomplishment. A superathletic accomplishment, like leaping 40 feet into the sky and floating down onto the rim, a play so superhuman in nature that I literally cannot imagine my awkward, slender body doing it. This game took me places where my imagination failed to go.

Christopher Nolan's 2006 film, *The Prestige*, defines a magic trick as a three-act structure. There's the pledge: a ground situation, a stable thing shown to the audience. There's the turn: all of the action, the story on stage, the sawing-in-halves & the disappearances-with-poofs. Finally, there's the prestige: the impossible thing done, the resurrection, the new stability.

> **"They're illusions, Michael."**
> —**Will Arnett**, *Arrested Development* (2003-2006, 2013)

Here is a partial list of illusions I have fallen for:
- Thinking that pumping the button on Reebok Pump sneakers would make me jump higher
- Thinking that Nike's Air Max insoles would make me jump higher
- Thinking that any of the Orlando Magic's draft picks would land them a franchise cornerstone
- Thinking that Orlando will ever win a championship
- Thinking that my ability to perceive reality was wrong,

during a psychology experiment I volunteered for in college, not knowing that the other "volunteers" were students in on the illusion, trying to throw me off with wrong answers to questions to see if I'd doubt myself.

- Thinking that my dad would never ever become sober & was therefore unworthy of love
- Thinking that I would grow up to be a video game designer
- Thinking that the place I'm from, and by extension myself, would be admired by others if a local sports team won a championship

"You wanna bet? 500 dollars? Shoot. You musta been watching 3-Card real close. Ok. Lay the cash in my hand cause 3-Card's the man. This card you say? Wrong! Sucker! Fool! Asshole! Bastard! I bet yr daddy heard how stupid you was and drank himself to death just cause he didn't wanna have nothing to do witchu!"
—Don Cheadle, *Topdog/Underdog* (2001)

We've all seen 3-Card Monte, or that trick where you follow the plastic cups. Something is revealed to you & you are asked to follow it, to never let it out of your sight. You're shown a 1995 NBA Finals appearance? You follow that card only to reveal Michael Jordan un-retiring. You follow that ball & what's under the cup is Shaq leaving for the Lakers. You're shown a star point guard with an unnatural combination of height and athleticism for the position? You're revealed knees that can only handle that torque for so many years before crumbling like the plastic that Lil' Penny was molded from. You're shown a do-it-all swingman in Tracy McGrady to rebuild the team around? You lock eyes with the red cup named "Playoff Victory" but it always, always comes up empty when you point to it. The dealer shows you a veritable Superman in Dwight Howard but the card you gamble on is more like Kal-El in Kansas—all the power but for all intents and purposes a baby. You keep picking out playoff failures. You keep picking out the Atlanta Hawks inexplicably shooting 70% from the field. You keep getting shown top-5 draft picks to rebuild the team with and you spend three years glaring at the dealer as he flips over tweeners who can't shoot. Your eyes follow every motion & movement and you still can't tell exactly how you fail but you always fail. What a hustle.

I don't like the current roster of the Orlando Magic. I don't like the organization's approach, its squandering of draft value, its complacency with losing, its inability to coach up talent, its lack of starting depth, its propensity to trade what talent does develop for draft picks in the future; a future which looks increasingly far away, a Zeno's Paradox on hardcourt. It's an honest question that I should've asked myself years ago, and am only going to ask myself now reluctantly: why am I still a Magic fan? I've never seen the Magic play in-person. I've been to Orlando once. It's been nearly 20 years since I've seen Penny and Shaq play together, but I still drink sadness beers as the Magic botch another playoff series. I still change my Xbox Live avatar's clothing to a Magic shirt every fall when the NBA season starts. I can still fire up *NBA Jam: Tournament Edition* on my Sega Genesis and put on a steals-and-threes show with Nick Anderson and Dennis Scott, absolutely refusing to play as any other team than the Magic. Why do this to myself? What am I loyal to?

I feel like I'm tricking you right now. Laying out thought after thought—memories & cultural artifacts juxtaposed—the section breaks acting as my own slight-of-hand. You're making what you think are connections but all of this is misdirection. Your connections are illusory; I'm not understanding anything new about myself at all.

I've been playing Magic: the Gathering since 1999. My core friends from high school, who I still consider to be my best friends, all played too. Playing Magic was the ostensible reason we had to get together during college, when we were attending different schools, when we'd each drive home to Excelsior Springs, MO, once a month or so. Even now, over five years since I graduated from college, I still want to play Magic with those guys. But we have careers now, mostly. We have responsibilities. Relationships. Children, in Derek's case. That familiar refrain. For a long time I really thought we were special. I thought we were the only old group of friends to never grow apart. I thought this card game was a literal spell, that we were bonded together through this force. It was my birthday recently and I didn't get a phone call from any of them. A couple of texts. That's okay; I forget about their birthdays too. This is very normal and yet I'm sad about it. This section could have been about even older friends and role-playing games—Black Mages and D&D campaigns and cycles of addiction—but that's familiar too. You know who the successful magicians are? The very few who come up with new tricks.

I'm the mark in this essay, not you. As always, I'm tricking myself with this line of thought about me and the Orlando Magic. I've been misdirected, looking at the wrong things. This isn't about the Magic. This isn't about videogames. This isn't about adolescence. What this essay really wants to be about isn't what this essay is about. What it's about is right there under my nose, and might even be on the page, but I didn't see it. I caught a glimpse of it but I don't want to type it out. It cuts too deeply. The essayist is the essay's worst enemy.

"Now you're looking for the secret. But you won't find it because, of course, you're not really looking. You don't really want to work it out. You want to be fooled."
—Michael Caine, *The Prestige* (2006)

[BRI]

NEW JERSEY NETS

I was born in New Jersey—you can hear it in my speech: how I pronounce *O*s as *A*s, how I add a letter to the word *both*, how *W*s find their way into words on nights that grow too long with gin. Nights I tell stories of missed shots all happened there: in middle school gymnasiums, in driveways where you couldn't shoot from the left baseline because if you missed the ball would roll down the hill to the forest.

My first basketball game was a Nets game. My father took me to East Rutherford to see the Nets play the Clippers. Our seats were behind the basket a few rows back—an angle I had never watched a game from before. The game always looked perfect from half-court as cameras tracked the ball wherever it went. It took me a long time adjust to this: how I was unable to keep pace, how the players looked different when looking at them head on, how they disappeared down the court and grew smaller.

My souvenir from the game was a coffee cup and Nets wristbands: the red, white, and blue logo, one for each arm. I remember crashing hands together, as if the wristbands gave me power—that I could be stronger than I ever have been, that I could fly, that I could read the minds of everyone within thirty feet. I could make every shot. I could stop the ball from rolling into the woods. I would eat ice cream out of the coffee cup, as I was too young for coffee, and sometimes feel as if I still am. This is what it is like to be a grown-up, I thought—to be old enough to appreciate a basketball game, to come home with something more than just a memory of what it was like; that carrying these thoughts with you will never be enough. We do this because, as we get older, we remember things incorrectly—we imagine things that were not there, give importance to the minute.

My first memory was holding onto the walls at my grandparents' house as I walked into the room where my parents were watching television. It is then I came to as a human, as if my body existed but the rest of me did not—as if someone pressed start and took over the role of the computer, replaced it with a live human whose patterns became more and more erratic. I remember wood paneling. My mother cannot pinpoint any of this; she does not remember who had this house—my grandparents certainly did not. I would provide more details, but I can't; my consciousness left the second the lights flickered on.

I am telling you this because there is a ghost in the machine. By the time the game reached peak popularity in late 1993,

Dražen Petrović was dead. Considered to be one of the greatest international players of all time, Petrović was killed in a car crash on the Autobahn during a rainstorm: a tractor-trailer lost control and the car Petrović was in crashed into the back of it, sending him through the windshield, his head smashing against the semi-truck's diesel tank.

I don't remember if I saw Petrović play that night—I cannot place how old I was, or what year my father took me. I might've gotten the coffee cup and wristbands on different trips—we saw a few games when I was younger, but they all blend together: the first time I saw the Celtics, the time I cried when my father's alma mater got blown out by North Carolina.

Petrović was removed from later releases of the game—his pixels swapped out for Kenny Anderson, the Nets' second-year point guard. The game, however, remembers Petrović; at random intervals, even when the Nets aren't playing, the announcer will shout his name, *Petrović!*, as if he is taking a long distance shot or rising up for a tomahawk dunk. In later iterations, when Anderson takes a shot, they'll shout out *Petrović!* as if he is hiding within the machine, waiting to be unlocked.

I am waiting for the moment that I come into being. There will be a moment at which I will lose all knowledge of everything that I have ever done. I will forget the names of those that I love; I will misremember what is in my heart and why it is there. The night that I misremember, I was there, waiting to bubble toward the surface, my hands running over the grooves in the wall. When you play the game you are two places at once: you are on the court and you are standing in front of the machine, as if you are shrouded in prayer. When you are playing, you are Dražen; you are unstoppable from the corner. When you are playing, you cannot leave the court—you are forever in the field of the game.

You try to run past the baseline and into the crowd, up the stairs of the arena. You do this to see if you are there, younger than you've ever been, pressing your wrists together, willing the ball to go in. Instead, your feet will pump up and down, yet they will never catch the ground. You will continue to do this until someone brings you back. Once you exist in a place, you can never truly leave. You will do this until someone calls out your name.

[BRI]

MIAMI HEAT

In basketball, there is something called a *heat check*—a ridiculous shot that you fire toward the basket to see how hot you are, to see if somehow you can transcend every single rule, as if you are blessed by something larger than how your wrist snaps on the follow through.

I wish I believed in transference: that things can be predicted, that if something is true one day, it will be true the next. I try to talk to myself into grandiose statements: that last game, I shot the ball well, so this game should be a continuation of successes, that if I eat the same breakfast, that if I listen to the same song, I have unlocked some key in the universe. I have let the ghost of times out of its box and it will guide the ball toward the hoop in a way that is has both remembered and has always been known.

This has happened twice in my life—where every shot went in no matter where I stood: that I was in a constant state of *heating up*, as the game barks anytime a player makes two baskets in a row. The first was when I had just gotten contact lenses—I had worn glasses since the third grade, where one day I was convinced that there was nothing written on the chalkboard: just a green blank with no notes. I did not realize that you could see other people's eyes from that far away—I thought that all faces were impossible things until seen from up close, that everything shifted into proportion the second I got closer; noses and cheekbones straightening themselves out like they were caught red-handed trying to stray.

I wish I could tell you it was because I saw better—that when I first put the lenses in I could see things in my periphery, that I could move my eyes around and my vision would never shift—everything would be as clear as crystal. All I needed was to be able to see better and I could transcend into greatness. Instead, I played the game with one eye clear and one eye blurry: while in putting my lenses in, I scratched my cornea with my fingernail—a sudden pinch, the whites in my eye filling up with blood, a constant tear building on the bottom lid. I would shoot the ball with one eye closed—it would roll over the front of the rim and in, as if I had figured out that my right eye had been betraying me all this time; that it was telling me that the world was one way when in fact it was the other.

The other time is when I was older: I left a girl in my bed to go play basketball. Her, possibly still drunk from the night before, and me, stubborn in my routine. I arrived at the gym ready to tell stories to my friends—about how you couldn't believe what I had done, that I had made the wrong choice in playing, that I was bad at decisions, because here I am, and there she was, asleep. That this somehow made me more masculine: that I had chosen basketball over relationships, that this stuff happens all the time. That if it happened once, it could easily happen again.

There are nights when I go to my favorite bar and I play songs from my laptop—the lights are dimmed, whiskeys are shot back, and the dance floor gets sweaty with mobs of hormones, bodies slick and sticky. I like to think I've learned something over my years of doing this—of what songs get people dancing, of what tracks send people scattering to the bar to refresh their drink. However, there are nights when no one wants to dance—no matter the amount of alcohol, or how loud the PA rattles, everyone is there to stand around and talk about their day, who is here and who isn't, who is sleeping with whom. Songs that held an absolute truth fade into newer songs that cloy for a sudden rush to the space in front of the speakers.

Rony Seikaly, the Heat center in the game, has long since retired from basketball entirely—instead he puts all of his energy into music producing and DJing. After his retirement, Seikaly once said, "Sports will always be my love. But music will always be my passion." I will always love basketball—the sound that sneakers make, the smell of lacquered floor, the brightness of the whole spectacle. However, to say I have passion for it seems to be a lie. I was never a child who would shoot jump shots in the freezing rain; I never stayed after to practice further. Even now, I find myself choosing to sit at home with no music playing than to shoot around, to put shoes on, to drive to the gymnasium. Instead, I choose to live in the moments when anything is possible in hopes that I can make something permanent out of these swings of luck—that I've found something cosmic; that I know what song to play next and what eye to keep closed, that this half-love inside of me is somehow enough.

[BRI]

NEW YORK KNICKS

The cabinet for the game is a large imposing thing when you are young: a television screen larger than the one you have in the comfort of your own home, yourself on the tips of your toes so that you can reach the controls.

When the game is released you are nine years old. You are big for your age. You already know this. And yet the game seems so much larger than you are—it towers in ways you did not expect.

You and your mother would go grocery shopping. At the end of the cashier's line was a row of arcade games; all outdated, nothing fancy. To play the game, you'd have to go to the other side of the mall to the arcade with its dim lights and its teenagers: rumors and grandeur, drugs and cigarettes, grown men pretending to be boys.

You would take the quarters out of your mother's purse and you would play until you died or your mother had finished writing her check to the cashier. As a result, you'd play the games that had no story to them: a mouse being chased by cats, a circle being chased by ghosts.

When the game was released, it was expensive—25 cents could never do. Your mother refused to pay for more than one game; quarters became dollars all too quickly. It was almost impossible to play an entire game—you would pay by the quarter, the game begging for more credits despite having nothing to show for it, your pockets empty of everything except a Velcro wallet that held next to nothing.

You'd spend most of your time watching others play the game: kids with better haircuts and more tokens. The first time you played the game was at a birthday party where the game was unlocked and unlimited. You could play the game over and over and no one would say a word—there'd be no one to take your money; you could just hit start as many times as it was necessary. The other children went ice-skating. They jumped in ball pits, they ate cake. You, pressing start over and over again. You, down by three entering the fourth quarter.

When you got older, you went to Knicks games. You took the train in with your father, you emerged from underneath Madison Square Garden. You stood courtside; you saw how large these people loomed, how large the whole thing seemed to be: the undersides of scoreboards, the basket that somehow looked taller than the ones you shot at in the parks near your house. You read a story once, about how basketball players from

New York did not know how to shoot because the rims were too stiff. If the ball did not sail perfectly through the hoop it would ricochet out—it would rattle and spit. You think of how the Knicks in the game adhere to this stiffness: Patrick Ewing and his failing knees staying close to the basket, Charles Oakley only shooting the ball when grabbing an offensive rebound—his role to protect what he was told to hold dear at any cost. How large they were—how imposing. How their height did not match yours. How they were able only able to hold things if they held them close. How, no matter how large you are or become, you will always feel incomplete. You thought all of this despite being larger too: that you are a grown man, that you are no longer nine. You keep quarters in a jar in your closet. You can take the train by yourself.

The Knicks were perpetually one piece away: everyone playing their role, but coming up just short. There was something always missing, like they had run out of credits. There is a code in the game where you can make everyone's head grow: every head bobbling, everyone becoming more cartoonish than they've ever been. Your head is already large—even larger than your body. When you were a baby it would roll back—your neck not holding up the weight. The city too, is large—how everyone says it feels alive, how it never sleeps. To say this is to acknowledge that you are a part of something larger than who you are, that you are meant to fill gaps between buildings, be entrenched in the swarm of a sidewalk. You are here to save the world. You are here. You have run out of quarters. You are forced to watch the game slip away, clocks ticking until everything resets. You are so far away from competing. You must admit that you are not one piece away from greatness—that you are the piece that is missing.

A name. Mahmoud Abdul-Rauf. The pronunciation carves a cave out of sound, teeters on collapse, the lack of the fricative at the end of the name preventing the turn from pivoting on itself, until the sound ends, and the name you recited remains hanging in the air like some kind of eulogy to a vowel you didn't know you loved.

The world knew him first as I knew him as Chris Jackson. A sprite little shooter from Gulfport, he was the pinnacle of the Dale Brown era of LSU basketball. The college game in that era was entirely different than the game that we see now, with athletic teams pushing the floor, attempting to score as quickly as possible each

DENVER NUGGETS

PLAYER 2

[AAA]

possession, rather than the slow burn of the possession game that we now see.

I actually never saw him play for LSU, except on grainy Youtube clips while I lived in Baton Rouge. There was the game when Jackson went for 53 against Florida as a freshman. Or the game where he put up 55 against Ole Miss. He could dribble and drive, and he could step back shoot the three. Then there was 51 on Texas or 45 on Georgia. In only two years he averaged 29 points per game, scoring in double figures in 63 out of 64 games, with 52 games with more than 20 points, 28 games with more than 30 points, and 11 games with more than 40 points, and 4 games with more than 50 points. In short, he was one of the best college basketball players of that era. He was taken as the third overall pick in the 1990 draft by the Denver Nuggets, where he paired with players like Dikembe Mutumbo, LaPhonso Ellis, and Antonio McDyess on a high flying, yet consistently under-achieving team.

What I remember of college basketball in the early 90's was a particular event on ESPN, the exact name of which I cannot recall, though I do remember that it involved a between-the-legs dunk by J.R. Rider (before he became Isaiah) where you could call in and hear Dickie V's voice ask you who you thought had the best dunk. I remembered the number for years and called it every so often for no particular reason. Dickie V's voice answered with a recorded message, saying that the number was no longer working. I'm not sure if that part is true, whether it was from a dream I had years later, or if I did call the number and got the standard robotic response.

The type of game that Jackson played, the game that college basketball was in that era, formed the basis of my own hoop dreams. Teams seemed to push the floor with such a high tempo

that each commercial break and timeout was like a welcome re-
prieve that lasted long enough for the viewer to catch his breath
before it began again.

Watching Jackson at LSU evokes clichés of children on the
playground. Now that I'm old, sore, and injuries prevent the
same wanton disregard for my body, I long for the little green
space in suburbia, the empty court at the gym, the lonely dia-
mond baking in the sun with sawgrass growing in the outfield,
places where I can run and throw my body against an enemy, a
stranger, a friend who I knew only through sport, and run after,
under, and with a ball, to run without thought of my body failing me, without thought at all. The freedom with which children
express themselves might be the source of my nostalgia, but it
is also now the cynicism of adulthood I want to avoid, to juke,
to dribble, to run away from. Somehow sport has become less
exciting for me now that it means so much, now that I only have
time to watch the teams I choose to follow. I expect disappointment, I expect failure, I wouldn't know what to do with success
because I've felt it so rarely.

I think part of sport cynicism comes from watching my he-
roes fail, one by one and magnificently, so that I'm the only one
who seems to remember their name.

Mahmoud Abdul-Rauf. I only began to like him when he
converted to Islam. I now think it interesting that he changed
his name from Chris, short for Christopher, meaning *carrier of
Christ*, to Mahmoud, from the same triconsonantal root as the
name Muhammed. He traded one founder of religion for another when he converted, which makes me think that he was more
thoughtful about his name than I ever could be. In that way, I
think what he did was a powerful expression of the self. Instead
of choosing to go by a given name, he chose his own name, and

how he wished to be called in the world. How few of us can understand that sense of empowerment to dictate to the world the terms of expression, to name ourselves for the world. I've never thought about the difference between a name that is given and a name that is chosen. I imagine most of us have wished for a different name, so that somehow our life would follow the nominative determinism of our new name.

I remember little of him playing basketball. All I remember was him refusing to stand for the flag during a game. I told my father about it and asked him *why would a Muslim do such a thing?* I do not remember my father's answer. And even now I can't describe to you why I think of that move as a failure. Perhaps because it was so easily forgotten, or that it was a meaningless gesture in response to a meaningless ceremony. I honestly cannot remember. Perhaps I think it was because it did wash away what he did on the court or perhaps it was because he was braver than I ever was in that instance. I can't help but think of it as a failure, and since it is, I can remember nothing more of it.

All I remember is that one day he was Chris Jackson, and the next day he was Mahmoud Abdul-Rauf. One day, one life ended and another began.

[BRI]

MILWAUKEE BUCKS

Basketball is a game of statistics: everything is ascribed a number. We talk about these things when we make our points—someone else is counting for us. What we have seen means nothing compared to what has been tallied. The game has numbers as well, ways to let the player know what teams to embody and what teams to avoid. These numbers are garish: emphasis on speed and blocking ability, but also in how well one can dunk, how one can dazzle.

My first job was as a statistician for a men's basketball league in my hometown. I would sit at the scorer's table and tally points, keep track of the fouls. I knew these men by name:

I would see how they would play, I would know who would be getting the ball when the game was on the line. I would fill up the off-green pages with ticks: lines in pencil as official as any of this could possibly be—men past their prime crashing into each other's bodies, moving a step slower in galloping back down the court to play defense.

This is where I fell in love with averages: how, when you combine numbers and divide them, you can reveal some sort of truth—that outliers can skew good data raw, but everything will bounce back. I would take the books home and enter them into a spreadsheet—sort the points scored, send players' names skyward.

My father was the best player in the league. I do not have the data to prove this—the files long since archived, the ink smeared and the paper warped from a basement flood, the documents incompatible with new layers of technology. Even then, I could not prove this to you with numbers; I could only keep track of points scored, rebounds grabbed, free throws made. There was no concern for assists or steals, no plus-minus statistics, no field goal percentages. I could see how he played: how he moved in the lane, how he kept his eyes up, how he had a hand in the face of every opponent. Yet I wanted my father to score more points— to make real seem more real. I wanted him to take every shot, to shoot every three-pointer whenever he had a whisper of space, to break down my fourth-grade math teacher for the scoop and score. I wanted him to be the sum of his numbers—to forgo the open pass and pull up in transition, to be tangible.

Statistically, the Milwaukee Bucks are the worst team in the game: Brad Lohaus played for thirteen years and averaged less than six points; Blue Edwards was, at best, a role player on some historically awful teams.

There is nothing enticing here. The game, twenty-two years after its release, is a game of nostalgia. There is no driving force inside of us now that wishes to miss 18-footers off the back iron as a player who is at his best from beyond the three-point arc.

And yet, the Bucks could catch lightning in a teacup: Lohaus scored 34 points in a game once, Edwards recorded the first triple-double in Grizzlies history. We remember these anomalies: the numbers will always spring back to where they were supposed to be—a spike of brilliance, a valley of a shot gone cold. In the game, your player can *catch fire*—if they make three consecutive baskets, the ball turns into a smoking, glowing orb when in their hands. The ball has a much higher statistical chance of going in the basket. The nets burn with every shot made, each ember an acknowledgment of the perceived impossible.

One game, my father couldn't miss—he could hit every shot from every angle, his teammates passing the ball to him at every impasse they created for themselves, asking my father to do the unburying. Afterwards, as we drove home in his Buick Century, sweat soaking into the felt seats, I asked him why he couldn't do that every single game: the naivety of a child who does not understand how probability works, the audacious and beautiful belief that what is possible in one moment is possible forever.

[BRI]

SAN ANTONIO SPURS

Patterns emerge the more you watch the game. You notice that the CPU players like to run in loops in the back court, that they wait for the defense to collapse on one player before passing the ball to the other. You notice how they swing their elbows after grabbing a rebound if you lean too close to their bodies, how they always know when to jump if you attempt a shot from the top-left part of the key. When players rise up for a dunk, they go with their right hand raised: all thunder and power as they grab onto the rim. When they shoot from the outside, it is with the left hand: both hands raised, but one wrist cocked forward at the point of release.

My father was recruited to play basketball at the Air Force Academy out of high school. Gregg Popovich, assistant coach at the AFA at the time, and future San Antonio Spurs coach, picked him up at the Colorado Springs Airport. "It was the first time I've ever ridden in a Cadillac," my father said, when he told me the story many years later.

Flying an airplane is much like playing a video game—there is the sensation of controlling something much larger than you are: an embodiment of a vessel, a commanding of an internal and external space. There is movement and stasis: all things reactionary. The beauty of flight is repetition: to commit something to memory, to do things over and over until it becomes natural, but not too natural in order to let complacency slide in. This is how we lose planes. This is how the game catches up.

The beauty of David Robinson was in his patterns—how he would never flinch from his set-ness, how he treated all things like a task: a hold-over from his days in the Naval Academy with a love of proper order. Robinson was a leftie too. Despite being over seven feet tall, he was more at home from 22, forgoing monstrous dunks for a baseline jumper, or a lean-in bank shot.

Perhaps this is why he was called *soft* as a player—that he did not have the mental or physical toughness to bang bodies when it counted; his Spurs teams shrunk whenever they came up against the Rockets, were bullied when playing the Suns. He preferred the finesse from the outside, the posting up simply to face up, the driving of the lane only when the path was open.

Or perhaps it was because Robinson wasn't supposed to play basketball: as a high schooler, he quit the team more than once before being convinced that he was a natural, that his height was a gift from the gods, that all of this was meant to be, that left-handed shooters have an advantage in basketball because of their unorthodoxies, that no one can see someone like him coming. Instead, he was too tall for the Navy—his height preventing him from serving at sea—the diversion from a formation, an anomaly.

My father left the Air Force Academy after his sophomore year. His eyesight simply was not good enough to be a pilot—his photo after going through basic training shows him, face gaunt, with no glasses, as if to prove that they were not needed. He left the basketball team too. At just over six feet, he wasn't tall enough to break the rotation.

My father doesn't tell too many stories from his days at the Air Force Academy. I can see his blue jacket hanging in the hallway; I can see his *honorably discharged* certificate dated two years before his planned graduation date. One thing he told me about was the first time he did a barrel roll—how freeing it felt, how it was just like in the movies, how it was just like in a video game. How astonishing it must've been to have the power to be within a concept. The instructor then told him to do another: to spin the plane upside down, for only a moment. Then another. Then another. Then another.

[BRI]

INDIANA PACERS

All of my basketball advice involves imagination—the visualization of something that transcends the realm of reality. When I shoot a basket, I imagine a flash of water inside of my body, crawling up my legs and into my shoulders. I stab my toe into the ground to plant my foot—I draw the energy from the hardwood floor. I flick my wrist and the ball is let go—a body in motion propelling an inanimate object toward the basket.

My father's piece of advice for me when shooting baskets was to picture the ball going through the hoop. He would tell me to visualize the arc—the path that the ball would take as it left my hands—as if it were a taut string that looped towards the skylights and dipped down through the middle of basket. This is something that he did when he shot free throws—that he believed that there was no chance of the ball not going in; that if the ball rattled out or came short, there were other factors at work, that his will was strong, that he had already seen it happen, so it must come to be.

In later iterations of the game, there is a statistic that ranks *clutch*—meaning that players with a high ranking have a higher likelihood of a shot going in during the final seconds of the game. Reggie Miller made 21 game-winning shots in his career, including a 1995 playoff game against the Knicks during which he made eight points in nine seconds. In the game, Miller steals the ball on the inbounds pass after Greg Anthony falls down— the ball somehow floating into his hands before taking a dribble backwards, stabbing his right foot into the parquet floor, and tying the game. Miller's clutch statistic is one of the highest in the game—quantifiable proof that Miller can will the ball through the hoop, that it is written in the code.

Miller, of his ability to come up big late in games, said, "No matter how good you are, there's a lot of luck involved." This is something that someone who is good has the luxury of saying—that a player can give all of their glory to something larger than they are if they themselves can transcend what is expected of reality.

My father was once fouled on a three-point attempt with no time on the clock—his team down three. He needed to make three free throws in a row to send the game into overtime. I was there. I don't remember much from it except that the lights in the gym somehow seemed brighter than they usually were, that the reflections off the floor caused a glare. My father made all three baskets and his team went on to the championship game after winning in overtime. I told him that it was something that I could never do, that I would be the first to point fingers at another representative, that I was better off where I was—on the sideline, shielding my eyes from the shimmer, that I would've missed the shot before I was even checked the ball.

At my cousin's funeral, my father gave the eulogy. There was no other choice in the matter, because there was no one else who could've done it, who had the ability to step up and deliver. We have a hidden belief that to be able to come through in difficult situations is a quantifiable thing, that some people in this world have an ability to make a shot because it is what is asked of them in that moment; there is no thought that goes into dexterity at a certain moment—it just occurs because it needs to happen. To be a successful basketball player, you have to imagine things that aren't there. You have to see what will happen ahead of you— trust that when you pass the ball to an empty space, a teammate will be there to fill it with his open hands, and drive the ball through the hoop. In my sadness, I wanted to be that person: to write something beautiful, to stand in front of my family and my cousin's friends and deliver something transcendent, to see the arc of the universe, to see him sitting in the crowd. I still run through the funeral—how it would've went, how I wouldn't be able to make it through—that I would feel a hot burning on the side of my cheek, that the words would come out in breathy slabs of brick. I cannot picture it going any other way.

There are night animals in the shadows and the animals are humans and the shadows are cast by moonlight on the Ferris wheel and the humans are carnies smoking cigarettes outside our circus tent.

It is after midnight and the fair is closed. The front gates are locked. Tonight, like every night, we are still inside.

"Bring pepper spray and a knife when you walk to the bathroom," the fire-eater tells me as I leave the tent. "A switch blade is best," she says, "but a Swiss Army knife works too."

I'm new to the sideshow. My body is covered in snake scales after charming our 8-foot shedding beauty

GOLDEN STATE WARRIORS

PLAYER 2

[TGF]

all afternoon, so I thank the fire-eater and head to the showers even though I don't know much about the rules of this game.

"Oh and I wouldn't use nice-smelling shampoo and then walk back alone," she calls out after me. "I wouldn't do that," she says, and I thank her again, pass the carnies by the Ferris wheel and keep going.

The rules. There are the regular rules of the game and then there are cheat codes. My fellow performer is trying to give me some codes, but I was not a kid who grew up with video games and so I am never successful when I press the button I think I'm supposed to press the number of times I think I'm supposed to press it. I grew up with bok choy and that good hippie California belief in the power of tree bark and smiling and it was only through afternoons in the basements of a few friends' houses that I learned there were ways to change the rules, to become exceptional—if only I could learn the codes.

On the midway, the keys have been pulled from the rides and the lights flipped off and the barf scrubbed from the bucket seats. Looking at the undressed carnival feels like stumbling into a king's bedroom and catching him in dirty underwear. I hear no voices on the midway. I have no knife, no pepper spray. I'm close to the stuffed Angry Birds hanging by their necks from an awning, keeping near to avoid a few puddles in the center of the road. The bathroom is a six-minute walk. There are 160 carnies at this fair. My shampoo smells like coconut. I'm walking past the milk bottle toss, the goldfish game, the basketball shoot. I think my shoulder brushes an awning as I sidestep another puddle, my eyes sideways on the basketball hoop, but then all of a sudden no, it is not an awning, no, it's an arm reaching out at me through the darkness.

I am alone, I think, and panic.

I immediately revise: I am not alone.

A hand grabs my arm. "Hey girl," a voice says. A man steps out from behind the hanging row of stuffed basketballs. Cigarette. Sweat-stained baseball cap. Smooth, tight skin across his cheeks like someone is holding his head closed too tight from behind. He lets go of my arm to pull the cigarette out and exhale, and as he does, he smiles, a little pink tongue worming out the side of his mouth.

"I seen you," he says. "From behind."

My heart is kicking but I take a small step away and stand taller. His face is pink and sweaty. The basketball hoop behind him makes a halo above his head. *I am alone. I am not alone.*

In the basements, everyone wanted to be the Golden State Warriors. Our team. *NBA Jam* was the only game. "Can you even believe Malone?" the kids who knew which buttons to push and how many times to push them said and I nodded, watching. I could believe. With the ball, Karl Malone would weave through his enemies like they were statues, like it didn't even matter what threats they posed.

"How many seasons you been out?" the carnie asks and I want to lie, but don't.

"This is my first," I say. "First fair."

"Holy shit, a greenhorn. You won't ever be the same after this," he says. He has a thick southern drawl, so I ask him where he's from. I'm trying to play it easy, cool. I'm trying for codes.

The beat of a drum rises up from behind the curtain of rides and will probably maintain its dim beating all night, is sometimes still beating when "America the Beautiful" awakens me from the rodeo's loudspeakers each morning at 8:00AM. Whether the beat of this drum is from a party or malfunctioning ride or the rhythmic pound of another group of men breaking someone's bones, I never know.

"I'm from Atlantic City, New Jersey," he says, "but I put on a southern accent in order to catch these northern girls at the fair. They love the accent." He laughs, his tongue popping out the side of his mouth. "I know how to spot a true lady," he says, winking at me. The drumbeat gets louder. "My IQ is five points less than Einstein."

"I better get going," I say and start to step away, but his arm reaches out again toward my arm and I look around for the closest piece of metal or rock but find none. I wish I could say all of my brain wants to flee but the truth is this danger feels a little bit good and I know that that's trouble. I know I like feeling the rush of a threat. I know I always think I can beat it, that I can somehow juke whatever menaces.

"Wait," he says, stepping closer to my face, licking the edges of his mouth with his pointy tongue. "I'm gonna tell you something."

The drum beats on in the distance and the man's hand is on my arm and the gates are locked in a wide circle around us. I want to duck and fake like Malone. Instead, I pull my arm away.

"Easy there, I'm not gonna hurt ya," he says. "I just wanted to tell you. Do you know the secret to making hair grow longer?" he asks. I stare at him. Shake my head no. "Take calcium pills. Calcium is one of the key ingredients in hair," he says, coming closer until his mouth is pressed up close to my face. "Every chick wants longer hair," he whispers, his arm traveling up toward my hair, fingering the tips. From half court I'm alight and fly over my enemies, frozen statues, and spin 360 degrees in the air, one arm overhead as I tuck the ball into the hoop, as I've traveled more than six times my own body length through the night air and come home. Who I am here can be exceptional.

His hand is in my hair. My shower bag has a full bottle of shampoo, a full bottle of conditioner. I am sure I'll know what to do any second now. I am exceptional. I am standing on the midway. I cannot move.

"Well, I'll be seeing you," he says and turns to walk away. I do not move. I could alley-oop if I needed to. I think this again. If I really needed to, I could have flown fast away. "I'm quite sure I'll be seeing you," he says, his back to me, and he begins to whistle, the notes all wet in his mouth, and I'm standing still and also well above the rim, and the rain begins again, and in the next town over children are warm and asleep in their beds and a sheep in the barn down the midway begins bleating.

[BRI]

MINNESOTA TIMBERWOLVES

Every player dreams of making a game-winning shot: of releasing the ball a fingertip before the buzzer sounds, of winning the game, winning the championship, winning the heart of every person who ever lived in his city—of bringing something majestic home, of melting a winter with a fade-away. These were never things I dreamed of. My dreams were simpler: to have the ball in my hands and throw it as far as I possibly could—the time winding down, the ball bouncing into my hands, a heave of all my strength guiding the prayer up and over and through. It was all anyone wished for: to throw the ball from an impossible distance, to be completely reckless. It was not in the success, but in the attempt. Instead of strategy, it was simply desire: time is running out, there is no play to be drawn up for 2.1 seconds left, not with these weak arms and the length of the court to chew up.

It happened once: me, the biggest kid you've ever seen on the court, pushing the ball towards the basket. The ball seeming so close to going in—on target, yet my muscles having nowhere near the strength to get it close. Our eyes deceive us. It is how we believe that we are doing the right thing when we are doing the wrong thing. It's how we are able to remember things we never did and forget things that will always be written inside of our skin.

I would practice this shot—my cousin and I: we would have the gym to ourselves on hot summers in August; we would have the thrill of having an entire court to work with—not condensed to the driveway, no worries about losing the ball off the side of the rim and having it roll down the hill into the brush. I would miss left, always. He would miss right. We would always miss short, our arms and legs growing more tired, our overhand chucks becoming more erratic.

One time, we made three in a row: the first by chance, the second a miracle, the third something you'll never see again.

You will have to believe me. My cousin has been dead for twelve years.

If I knew this, I would've passed the ball more often—it only makes sense. A short shot is a perfect pass. This is how a different pack of wolves beat a juggernaut. This is why we know Christian Laettner's name, why he is on the Timberwolves: because there was the wherewithal to realize that a shot from half-court is impossible, that even if you make it three times in a row, there will be no one left to say they were there, that when the ball falls harmlessly in the key there's nothing left to say.

When playing the game, you will hit the wrong button. Your player will jump, leg out-stretched, and fire the ball towards the basket. The ball will go in more times than you can ever guess. Other times it will bounce unceremoniously off the backboard and spin back to you with a quickness. It will never fall short—it will never droop in a downward arc; it will never float towards the left or right side of the basket. It will always hit something. It will always come back. Don't try—please, just believe me.

[BRI]

CHARLOTTE HORNETS

The Hornets were new when I was young: the conflation of bees with something grander, a beautiful swarm of what it meant to be alive—the teal and purple on every heart of every child in every lunch room, coats draped over shoulders when the weather turned cold; mothers heading north on the highway to get discounts on outerwear, every child a fashion statement, every piece of clothing a statement of where they have come from, shiny and new, the world abuzz with the belief that the world would deliver us something larger than who we are. Beauty would rise up beyond consciousness: we could live and love without the reaction of humanity; we could fly; we could somehow be above the dirt in which we rose from.

My grandfather took measurements of his children. He predicted how tall they would grow to be, often with surprising accuracy. My grandfather did the same for me, believing that I would grow to be the tallest in the family. This is what I dreamed of: being the tallest person in the room, being the age that I was but towering over everyone—every child in a nylon jacket buzzing about their love of a team that they have never seen with their own eyes, from a town that is hundreds of miles away. I was stalwart in my love of my team. The antics of Larry Johnson as Grandmama did not phase me. Basketball was meant to be taken seriously, it was not meant to be mocked by grown men in dresses, trying to pass themselves off as someone older than who they were. I was never one who believed in growing older—I feared the future, how it sprawled out in front of me—that everything could simultaneously be finite and forever.

In the game, there is a turbo meter, a gauge that shows how long your player can run at full speed before tiring out and returning to the pace of what the world expects of us: feet sprawling in front of us in ways that seem remarkably human, nothing supernatural, nothing to take note of on cold nights where anything is possible.

The Celtics were playing the Hornets when my favorite player's meter ran out—completely blanked by circumstance, a fast start nullified by a collapse at half-court, the digital avatar just fading into oblivion. The game continued on without him: all flash and live and let live, a heart giving out for a brief moment, an anomaly in the grand scheme of things: fatigue, a hiccup, nothing that anyone should be concerned about.

He was unstoppable for the first quarter: ten points in three minutes, guns blazing, all energy and speed. He disappeared in the left corner of the screen, a slow jog that turned into a full-forward collapse. The announcers thought he was hurt, that his knee had buckled. Instead, it was written off as a moment of overexertion, a body not being able to keep up with the confines of itself.

There is a code in the game to give your player unlimited turbo: that the pace of the game quickens—that your fingers are perpetually holding down the button to go faster, as there is no reason to ever let up, to ever give anyone a rest. The game is not real, you say. You are not forcing blood to pump too fast into a web of coding; you are not forcing the heart to work overtime to compensate.

I have played games in which I felt I was going to collapse—that this was the end of days, that I had stopped growing, that my heart would simply give out from working too hard. I believe that there is something that is waiting to burst. We are alive as long as our mechanisms are in constant motion—our blood beating like wings. When our bodies are abandoned, we turn to paper: we dry up, we are left to be scattered on the wind. We must embrace our new concept of being limitless. We have no other choice.

WINTER BOYS

The boys fell out of me like winter.

An avalanche.

A hailstorm.

A flurry.

A snowfall.

All of the things cold and pouring that cover and destroy.

All boys.

They came with names lettered bold and high across their backs. Names like *Baylor*, *Horry*, *Nixon*, *Worthy*, *Wilkes*, *Fox* and *Fisher*. Names like *Lovellette* and *McAdoo*, *Thompson*, *Mikkelson*, *Gasol*, *Baylor* and *Chamberlain*. Names like *Odom*, *Hairston*, *Green*, *Scott*, *O'Neal*, *Johnson*, *Scott* and *Abdul-Jabbar*. I added their firsts, scrawled

LOS ANGELES LAKERS

PLAYER 2

[X T X]

them into the Champion Log and first-submitted them to the Deeming Board as was proper.

This was my second whelping so I knew more what to expect. I let them roam over me, feeding when they wanted, for as long as they wanted. A soft brown-white blur. I permitted them to fight one another for the breast. I didn't separate them as I had done with the others, before. Those boys all traded for trivial futures, I wanted higher for this lot.

I read books, articles, studies, and followed everything to the letter. And here they were, already a collective 60 pounds and 72" above my first whelping from the moment they hit the chamber's floor.

As the weeks passed, my mass whittled while theirs doubled. The infants wrestled and drained, wrestled and drained. Their largesse required additional aides who came to fuel, clean and turn me more than twice what was normal.

"Big bunch!" they'd say, impressed. "Team stock, eh?"

"I hope so! Put it as first choice into the Champion Log. We'll see."

Affirmative speculation abounded.

Thirty-three weeks brought boyhood. The Deeming Board had posted their first evaluation and it was as everyone predicted. I brought the boys their balls.

They fought for these harder than they'd ever did the breast. The nubbed, orange-brown rubber erupted a fever inside of them. Aides had to be called in. There was blood, broken bones. Separation was required; segments built with whomever would play well together. The groupings shifted and changed to bring new challenge, develop new skills. Three years later, when manhood arrived, the brood was ready to be parsed and sent. Their destiny—as predicted—the court.

The Deeming Board's fourth evaluation selected Lakers as

their designated purpose. I was thrilled. As the birther, my freedom was the sending. Who would go and when. They were mine
to do with whatever I pleased. A privilege given to each birther.
It was why I'd worked to bring boys. Warrior-ready boys who
would grow to warrior men. This flagon of fighting flesh all I'd
dreamed of since beginning my special path.

I needed to be with them first—all of them—before I began
their sending. A perversion long dreamt about. Yearned for.

I gathered them. A humid summer night that sat still and
waiting. The birthing chamber where they'd first arrived. I lay
down on the thick padding, my gown loose and falling. I ordered
them and they obeyed, fighting as they never had before, yet dis-
playing a synchronized teamwork they'd become dominant at.
So many of them it became a blur. They took me countless times.
I wore raw. Covered and destroyed. Winter once more.

I began sending the very next day. Ten of the best went first.
The ones I knew were most ready; Mikan, Mikkelsen, Nixon,
Lovellette, Chamberlain, Abdul-Jabbar, Johnson, Baylor, Hairston, West and Wilkes. Spent from the night before, the fare-
wells were terse and business-like. I would never see them again,
as was customary.

The balance thickened with their training. Their legs trunked
and sinewed under shorts that went from short to long to longer. I loved to watch the way they moved. The speed and dart of
them. The choreography of their plays; well rehearsed. My danc-
ers! The swan-like motions of their arms both male-strong and
female sway at the same time. When their needs came, I let them
come to me at will, encouraged and still dripping with sweat. My
winter. My Lakers.

I began dispensing here and there. The years were going by
and I knew if I were to have one last whelping, this batch would

need to be gone. But it was hard. Affection—discouraged but still there and true—had developed. The delegating was sporadic and abrupt, but it was what needed to be done.

McAdoo, Green, Cooper and Scott; this release, a sad one. We were five together for four nights preceding their placement. The first two nights, the remaining ten pounded the door, jealous with wanting, the sounds taunting a fever within them. The last two nights, the door was quiet, the brood having accepted the futility. After the four left, the ten pouted, scorned. I explained to them there were four less to have to share with, and when it was their turn to go, we'd spend the same special time behind chamber doors. This lightened them quickly and the days went by as before.

The remaining went in three batches. Thompson, Worthy, Horry and Fox were first. Four nights spent with the four of them, one night with Fox, alone—his fair face being one of my most favorites. The door stayed quiet throughout, the others knew they would get their turns soon enough.

The second batch of O'Neal, Odom and Gasol had their nights cut two short; their sizes more than I could handle for the promised four. The leaving was abrupt and shoving, the air of it slighted and bitter. I had no sufficient words for them.

The third and last batch was a mourning of sorts. I knew these were my last and so I had them abstain from practicing for their remaining days and instead, fall under my seclusion. It was only two—Bryant and Fisher—but being with them knowing they were about to be sent was a tiny death. There had always been something special about them; the glint in Bryant's eyes, his prowess on the court, the delicate round of Fisher's lips, his smile. I had grown extra fond of these ones, despite my attempt to keep platonic, as was a birther's goal.

We had our ways with each other. So many ways. And then they were gone. My last.

I have yet to come into another whelping. I am through with boys. I'm reading on the methods to achieve girls. I'm hoping females will come like summer—easy and free. I cannot have another winter. I am not strong enough. I cannot endure another winter coming hard then leaving me cold and alone.

[BRI]

CHICAGO BULLS

My father always told me that you need to go out on a make: that you can't leave the gym on a missed shot. It can't be something easy, either: it has to be from the free-throw line or better—no layups, no easy bank-shots from six-feet out. You will stay out there if it takes all night, if you have to. You will eventually will one in.

While recounting the story of his game-tying free-throws to my mother, my father admitted that he thought he missed the final shot, that he had short-armed it, that he could picture the ball resting for a brief second before falling back toward the floor, that he got a lucky roll. The game would've been over: there would be no chance for a put-back, no miracle shot to try to get the game back to where it should be.

I shoot baskets until my arms are tired and my fingers have gone numb from the cold. My forehead is dirty from wiping the sweat with my blackened fingers—each bounce kicking up more dirt from the asphalt. I will miss, and I will miss again.

And then you will make a shot that you have no business making: a heaved prayer turn-around from the corner that felt electric from the second you let it go—your body working like a pendulum, your wrist out, forward, pointed at the basket. You will laugh, shake your head, and chalk it up to luck, even though, in your heart, you know that the absence of something has the greatest presence.

You remember that on a shot chart, a make is counted as a zero—a void, a beautiful roundness containing nothing. It is pure in its construction—the image of a basketball, grown flat from the cold air, sailing through a hoop with no net. The made shot makes no sound—it does not rattle through, no swish—no cheers from the stands, no buzzer echoing. But it went in, and, for once, you can keep this pact—one made between all that remains and the enduring and beautiful weight of silence.

[BRI]

WASHINGTON BULLETS

The game is an experiment in duality. Basketball is not meant to be played like this. One-on-one is the game that romance was based upon: sons challenging their fathers, fathers using their height to grab every missed shot. 3-on-3 is how the game evolved when exchanging hardwood for blacktop—a natural half-court game when the other half of the pavement is taken up by kids like me hitting the underside of the rim. Two-on-two was never the plan. When the game was pitched, it was meant to be five-on-five, regulation—as realistic as we can possibly get, a true simulation. It is because of the game we use the word *arcade* to describe anything less real, yet more hyper-real: fewer players but with more muscles, rocket-boots for cleats, zero gravity. A world that runs parallel to our own.

Two-on-two is a game of absences: friends who promised to show up decided to go to the movies instead—their parents refusing to give them a ride down to the park. You can't run fours—you'll get blown off the court by the kids with the Air Maxs that flop out from the ankles. You never have the right shoes—never the ones that lit up, never the pumps, never anything but white-on-white, scuffed to hell, grass stains on the toes because this is the world you lived in and you wouldn't dare go barefoot.

The game is a game of twos. You buy the game for the dunking: the ability to do flips in the air that could never be imagined, to leave from the free-throw line and spin like a figure skater, to deliver the ball with a satisfying *chunk*. To rack up twos after twos, to try to pull off something that has never been seen before, that if you press the buttons at the right time, you can rotate for one extra spin. There were rumors that you could dunk from half-court—that your character could leap the length of the screen—nothing could get in your way. There were rumors about a lot of things, which never stopped us from trying to unlock every nuance: how certain players couldn't dunk, how every layup and finger roll was an insult to the game.

Here's how you win at the game: you do not dunk the basketball. You do not select the biggest stars, you do not try amaze your friends with what the game leaves up to chance. You shoot three-pointers—you counteract every dunk with a long shot from a short porch. Here's how you win at *NBA Jam*: you shove every player that comes near you. There are no fouls here; there is no blood. There are no free throw attempts, no stoppage in play, no time outs, no chances to catch your breath. You take every extra one you can get.

The Washington Bullets have no wonder. The following year, they will have Chris Webber, and the kids will have his shoe: the ones with a rat's tail down the side. Here, we have a recycled sprite: Harvey Grant, twin brother of Horace. Harvey wore goggles too, though they were not his signature look—that was already reserved for Horace, slyly putting his finger on every fault.

When the Bulls play the Bullets, all you hear is Grant—the name repeated in the same frozen exclamation, every crackled bark a repetition of what came before. It's the voice that is haunting. The fact that two people can look identical seems like an act of science, whereas two people sounding the same seems otherworldly—like some unholy transfer. My grandmother is a twin: when I was a child I would stare at my grandmother's sister despite only meeting her for the first time a few minutes earlier. I can tell the difference now: my grandmother's voice higher, her hair a bit taller.

I wore goggles, too: my glasses were too often knocked off of my head on an errant elbow, which sent them skidding across the gym floor. The best game I ever played was with one eye open—my right-eye scratched by a fingernail, the white turned red. I got every roll, every spin in my direction.

In a year, Harvey is gone, where Horace stays: replaced by Chris Webber, who is traded from Golden State. The Bullets, soon, will be gone as well: the owner believing that bullets are violent things that kill people in his city, that the murder rate is too high, that the only thing that can save everything is some sort of mystic shift beyond the power of having two people exist in the world with the same body. The logo is replaced by a singular being: a wizard mid-finger roll, insulting all that we know of the game. Gone is the logo: two hands coming out of the twin Ls, reaching towards the ball: either to receive it as it comes down off the rim, or being thrown forward toward the sky, a prayer on the sky wondering if it will be granted.

Once, I met almost the entire 92-93 Cavaliers team. I was having a birthday party at The Cleveland Metroparks Zoo. The players happened to be there with their families touring the brand new rainforest exhibit. My friends, great chums that they were, got all the players to sign something for me. But all I can remember is looking at fire ants while standing next to Larry Nance, who sort of looked at the swarming ants and then the swarming children and said, "Someone needs to get these damn kids outta here."

Memories.

That might seem like a strange anecdote, but CLE sports is weird,

CLEVELAND CAVALIERS

PLAYER 2

[SCK]

man. It's like a theater of the absurd or a grand guignol or maybe Samuel Beckett with whoopee cushions. It doesn't ever feel too far from the reality of *NBA Jam*. I mean, if I was watching the 2001 Cavaliers play the 2001 Lakers and Kobe's shoes caught fire and he dunked from the 3-point line, I would probably just fall back onto my couch, throw my hands up and say, "Ohh, of course he does it against us!"

So there we are, Cleveland fans, eternal vaudeville straight man to the cosmic comedy of sports. Would it surprise me if we played the Knicks and, for some reason, Warren Moon was running point? No. Would any of us be truly shocked if, in game, The Bulls subbed in their actual mascot who torched us for a triple-double? Maybe, but we would only blame ourselves. It's conditioning. Though sometimes a truly great team breaks through all that bullshit. And the team that *NBA Jam* used in its first incarnation represents a huge peak for my town, my team, and my fragile psyche.

The 1986 NBA draft might be the single best draft any Cleveland franchise has ever had. In that draft, Cleveland walked away with Hot Rod Williams, Ron Harper, Brad Daugherty and Mark Price. You're looking at every major Cavalier record holder in just about every major Cavalier statistical category for the next 20 seasons. That's amazing. Six years later, Williams, Daugherty and Price would send Larry Bird packing in his final playoff appearance. That happened just before Michael Jordan dropped a fucking cartoon anvil on all of them. You might have heard about it. The Cavaliers wouldn't go that deep into the playoffs for another 15 years.

But they would return, in 2007, which was awesome. And that Daugherty/Price pairing is, for my money, a top-10 *NBA Jam* duo. It might be top-5 in the original game, falling a few spots in T.E. because of a really weak bench. But when *Jam* was huge, and I was young, those guys were fun to watch. More importantly, they were fun to play as. You could go on a family vacation to your cousin's house in Baltimore and let that low-down-no-good-frontrunner play as the Alonzo Mourning/Larry Johnson Charlotte Hornets. They of countless *NBA Inside Stuff* montages. And you could take those guys down.

Price was quick, highly flammable and just stroked 'em from the baseline. Daugherty could dunk, play defense, and sported *Jam*'s most creep-worthy mustache. If you code-in legal goaltending this duo becomes almost unstoppable. All you really need to do is play Daugherty on defense and grab anything anyone shoots.

Which brings me to my dirty little secret. It really isn't that bad being a Cleveland professional sports fan. Yes, it would be easier other places. We tend to have a lot of plays that are named. That can't be good. You never want to be a part of too many of those. And with how many plays occur in a given year in all of sports you usually only see one or two per year get a name: "Music City Miracle" or "Immaculate Reception". So like, yeah, I wish we had less plays that stood out so much they deserved their own signifier. Still, we have so much sport in Cleveland. We overflow with sport. Northeast Ohio has 4.5 million people. Cleveland only has 390,000 people. And we have *three* major clubs. All your sport are belong to us.

You could argue we've been very irresponsible with all this sport. One might be tempted to say we are a reckless, drunken, bi-polar mess when it comes to how we use sport. And yeah, that sounds correct because, sports wise, we get pretty *Grimm's Fairy Tales* pretty regularly. I've grown to love it. With the Worldwide Leader spitting out piles of garbage trying to control the narrative of sport, it is refreshing to live and cheer in a city where the common rules and tenets of sport warp into the burned out magical husk of Pee-Wee's Playhouse.

Nothing sports in Cleveland is safe. 4th quarter leads? LOL. Once in a generation talent[1]?. Did your town have a weird television show where a guy in makeup showed horror and sci-fi movies at strange hours on local TV? Cleveland had one in the 60's and his name was Ghoulardi. We won our last championship in 1964. Ghoulardi went off the air in 1966 and—while it isn't true—it's probably true that he just took his alternate dimensions, UFO's and grease paint and slathered it all over the destiny of Cleveland sport before receding back into Lake Erie, cackling like a mad man. How else can you explain the story of Orlando Brown, of the Cleveland Browns, who once got hit in the eye with a penalty flag? The injury *ended his career*. That's some evil genie-type shit right there.

But hear me out, because I have some stats—and this was genuinely a pleasant surprise. Over the 33 years I've been alive in what is reportedly the worst sports town in history, there have only been *nine* seasons in which at least one of Cleveland's major sports clubs *didn't* make the playoffs. By my count those years were; '81, '83, '91, '00, '03, '04, '05, '11, '12. And it is tough to count '03-'04 because that was LBJ's rookie season, which, if you were around, was pretty special to see. And, if you want to cheer for Ohio State, as most of my Cleveland sisters and brothers do, you'll find a BCS National Championship in 2003, a Liberty Bowl victory in 1981, and *two* bowl wins in 2004 (Fiesta on Jan. 2 and Alamo on Dec. 29). It hasn't all been pretty. In fact, it has been carnival-freak-show ugly. But, don't let our gaunt faces and funnel cake bellies fool you, we've had some good times.

---

1 (fart sound)

Which brings me back to those 1986-1993 Cavs. They were probably the first team I ever loved. I wasn't really old enough to appreciate the gravity of the Browns. I just knew they gave my parents migraines. I played basketball, I knew the rules, and my team was pretty good. Did I ever get to see them? No. They played at the Richfield Coliseum, also known as the "The Palace on the Prairie." All of that information is true, but even the truth is a massive lie. The name "Coliseum" conjures images of Roman grandeur. The reality was a large, brutalist cube. It was far from a palace. And Richfield, Ohio, is not part of the majestic American prairie. The place is mostly woods. Once the arena closed, there were rumors they might turn the place into a prison. That's what we call a Cleveland knee-slapper.

However, while it stood, starting in 1986, the Coliseum hosted some incredible basketball. Likely forgotten by all but die-hard basketball fans, the late 80's early 90's Cavs were super legit. Over ten years they only missed the playoffs only once. They went to the Eastern Conference Finals twice. Three of those years saw 50+ win seasons. Watching Mark Price win three-point contests was, as a child, amazing. It was crazy. We had a guy in a contest and the guy won? *How is that possible?* But it's Cleveland and it's hilarious because those money balls looked like they were taken straight out of a rigged carnie game. But Mark played in the funhouse, so he knew how to hurl those wobbly, over inflated oblong spheres better than anyone.

Daugherty hung it up at 28, a five-time all star. His style of play was so non descript and so good I can't even really remember how he scored all those points. I mean, the guy only played eight seasons and retired the Cavaliers all-time leading scorer *and* rebounder. He was like Tim Duncan but human and not some kind of poorly wired sports robot whose prime directive is *take umbrage.* Wikipedia provided me with this amazing factoid about Brad. I have no way to easily include it so, thump, here it is. He selected his number, 42, as a tribute to NASCAR legend Richard Petty. That's so great! That feels like a small piece of goodness Cleveland willed unto itself. Like we all took a deep breath before that draft and were like, this #1 pick is going to be a good guy who respects others and pays tribute to that. Because we deserve some good stuff. Abracadabra. Brad Daugherty.

It's fitting that one of the few things I did see at The Richfield Coliseum was a Ringling Brothers circus. Because that's what sports is here—a goddamn circus. Only, it skews toward the tragic-comic. So when I am playing *NBA Jam* as Price and Daugherty, and they are tired because my bench is awful, and those goddamn Hornets come back from 25 down and beat my guys with an Mourning to Johnson 3-point line alley-oop I feel right at home. But don't feel sorry for me. I'll turn on cheats for the rematch and crush those fools.

[BRI]

SEATTLE SUPERSONICS

Gary Payton is not in the game. I am telling you this because you remember him in the game, but you are mistaken. He is nowhere to be found. You remember how fast he was, how he felt as if he had unlimited turbo. He could swing his arms and send the ball flying. You remember his shoes lighting up green as he tossed the ball to Shawn Kemp for a monster dunk. You remember that Michael Jordan is not in the game, but that is where you stop. You can picture Payton's digital face as you hover your cursor over the Seattle SuperSonics. You can see him lined up on the left, Shawn Kemp on the right, a giant green and yellow logo of a basketball with a Space Needle skyline in the middle. You remember thinking that Shawn Kemp could dunk the ball from the three-point line, but he couldn't. You remember a lot of things about the game that are not true. You remember a lot of things that are not true.

A tornado destroyed thirty percent of my town in 2011. There are a few things that I remember, but others I do not; there are days when everything runs together like flood water—everything a swirling trickle until something substantial is caught in the drift. I misremember the day the storm came as a Tuesday when it was a Wednesday. I drank coffee that morning; I met with students; I ate a lemon pastry. When the power was out and we did not know that almost half the town was missing I turned my attention to basketball: I would check scores on my phone; I would see the box scores pile up. I saw my team's lead diminish as I prayed for the numbers to somehow shift in my favor—that I deserved something like this, that I had been through enough that day, that I had hid underneath a mattress in a hallway, that the storm owed me this. I watched as the lead shrank to a deficit and the game ended. I remember that.

When my roommate told me he had cancer, we played video games. We played the game on broken controllers. In this version, there was Gary Payton—a member of an All-Star team, yet not as fast as we thought him to be in our youth. There was a desire to beat something—to have dominance over an inanimate object while bodies were not to be trusted. We watched bad television and ate junk food. Basketball did not save us, but the game might have helped keep us afloat.

I talked myself into this idea that basketball somehow owed me something: that on my darkest days I could turn to it, that my willpower in the world means more than what is tangible and measurable, that my loss weighs more than what anyone else could muster. The day my cousin died, I listened to the Celtics get eliminated from the playoffs on the radio in a parking lot outside of a liquor store. My uncle was buying beer for everyone—he bought more than even he could carry. When the game ended, I knew that the day had no chance to be redeemed, as if a game could bring back a life, could untie a noose, could bring us back to that gymnasium where we heaved the ball from half court. Even then, we were in charge: there was at least a small chance that something we did could make the ball go through the hoop. We turn to a game that we have no control over when we have no control over the world around us.

There is no team in Seattle now—they were swiped away in the middle of the night and moved to Oklahoma City. The SuperSonics, who had become the Sonics in later years, are now the Thunder: a visual representation rather than phenomena of speed and sound.

They have rebuilt most of my town: there are still pockets of overgrown weeds where trees used to be, although the new buildings, with their glass windows, reflect the glare into my eyes while driving to buy groceries. My roommate is cancer-free; we exchange text messages on the day of his yearly checkup. Every year, Seattle is rumored to get a new basketball team. They will be the Sonics again; they will be green and gold. I see my cousin in my dreams, as alive as the day he left us: he has just walked up the stairs from the basement where we used to stay up all night playing the game. It as if nothing ever happened; we continue on, the game ends and we have lost, but we re-enter our initials and give it another shot, as if he has been alive all of these years and I have been here alone and misremembering.

[BRI]

PHOENIX SUNS

My father saw him play once—at the Garden, a few seats from the floor. The tickets were given to him by his best friend in high school—the one who drove him to my mother's house and left him there without a ride home, forcing him to ask her on a date. He scored a double-double and got ejected in the fourth quarter—anything you could ever want from him: dominance followed by implosion—sun sphere, dark matter.

I met him in the Birmingham Airport as I prepared to fly home for the first time after moving to Alabama. I recognized him from down the terminal: nylon track pants, a black Nike hat pulled low over his eyes. It was the way he walked that drew my attention—stiff-kneed and upright, the inevitable breakdown of a body accelerated by the sheer amount of steps logged, inches jumped.

If you asked me who I most wanted to be like, it was him. A round mound of rebound, a supernova, a bowling ball with sparkling backspin. He destroyed Godzilla. He dunked over players taller and more athletic—those tan bag-of-elbows boys who could outrun me, who could dribble with both hands, who could keep their eyes forward instead of waiting for the next up-bounce.

I too believed that I was a great player on the wrong team, a sideshow in every way. I could be the best if I just got the ball, I thought—each slick point guard dribbling themselves into a corner, never looking toward the middle. I was useless because I kept my back to the basket; by the time I turned around, it would be too late—the ball stripped from my hands and sent back down the court—myself the fool.

He remained an uncrowned champion—his teams consistently falling short. Here is someone who gave his life to basketball, yet basketball did not give him back anything but sourness.

I don't know which game my father saw. I have looked through old box scores to see if the stats line up, but I have difficulty finding the right game. There are a few it could be: games where he got 20 and 10 but was never ejected, others where he got T'd up but barely got up enough shots.

Here's what I tell people when I tell this story: I tell people that we talked for the entire flight—that we shared stories of our own fathers, of how my father saw him play some unnamed night where he stole the show, of the universe and all its inconsistencies, of living in Alabama at a time when the blacktop being cracked and overrun with grass is the least of its problems.

Here's what I will tell you: I was too nervous to talk to him, to tell him that, despite his shuffle, despite the soreness, I would've given anything to be that, just for one day—spinning off of any and everything on the way to an easy lay-up. I asked the flight attendant to get me an autograph. He signed an Alabama postcard, a souvenir I was bringing home to New Jersey—a clever thing, a way to make it seem like my new home was temporary, a quick stop before the world brought me to where the world needed me. I thanked him as he was waiting for his bag. I shook his hand and he asked me why I was in Alabama. I told him I was in graduate school in Tuscaloosa, and he told me I was at the wrong school, that I should be at his alma mater across the state. I laughed; he wished me a Merry Christmas.

On the postcard, he signed *Best Wishes*, as if he knew that I could do better than my childhood prayers, that he was not someone to embody, that instead of spending my days in front of a television pretending to be someone else, that instead of spending my days in a driveway pretending to be someone else, that instead of spending my days in Alabama pretending I was somewhere else, that there was something else: some grand, blinding, imperfect else.

ABOUT THE AUTHOR

Brian Oliu is originally from New Jersey and currently teaches at the University of Alabama where he directs the Slash Pine Press internship. He is the author of two chapbooks & the full-length collections *So You Know It's Me* (Tiny Hardcore Press, 2011), a series of Craigslist Missed Connections, *Leave Luck to Heaven* (Uncanny Valley Press, 2014), an ode to 8-bit video games, and *i/o* (Civil Coping Mechanisms 2015), a memoir in the form of a computer virus. He is working on a series of lyric essays on professional wrestling as well as a memoir about translating his grandfather's book on long distance running.

ACKNOWLEDGMENTS

Sections from Enter Your Initials For Record Keeping appear in different forms in the following journals:

"New Jersey Nets/Los Angeles Lakers," *The Butter*

"On The False Duality of *NBA Jam* and the Grant Brothers," *The Destroyer*

"Undeliverable as Such, or, What You Need to Know if You Select the Utah Jazz in *NBA Jam*," *Thumbnail 6*

"New York Knicks," *Midway Journal*

"Sacramento Kings," *Stirring*

"Philadelphia 76ers," *Miracle Monocle*

"Detroit Pistons," *Pinball*

"Orlando Magic," *Everyday Genius*

"*NBA Jam* is not what you remember, but nothing is," *Polygon*

"The Milwaukee Bucks and the Statistical Outliers of Admiration," *The Mondegreen*

"San Antonio Spurs and the Beyond Yet Under Our Control," *Cartridge Lit*

"All Timelines for the Minnesota Timberwolves Relate Back to Someone Named Kevin" by Tasha Coryell, *DIAGRAM*

"John Starks" by Salvatore Pane, *American Short Fiction*

I would like to offer thanks:

To editors who published these essays and commented on them graciously or critically: Roxane Gay, Nicole Chung, Andrew Schenker, Christopher Lowe, Sarah Einstein, Dominic Gualco, Ben Kuchera, Bobby Rich, Lucas Church, Matt Sailor, Justin Daugherty, Joel Hans, and all of the assistant editors who helped make these pieces game ready.

To Jill Talbot, Justin Carter, David LeGault, Paul Arrand

Rodgers, Michael J. Wilson, Daniel Wagner, Marc Torrence, and Sam Martone for looking at beta glitched out versions of these essays.

Special thanks to Elizabeth Wade for always knowing what I meant to do on that last possession and helping me get there.

To the folks at Cobalt Press for being incredible editors and publishers and for your court vision. I am forever indebted to y'all.

To Gabe Durham for putting the first quarters up.

To all of my player 2s for agreeing to join me on this wacky experiment, especially Jason McCall, who put up with me talking about this project over fried chicken every Sunday for three months.

Special thanks to Salvatore Pane and Aubrey Hirsch who got this ball rolling.

To anyone who got excited when they heard that I was writing a book about *NBA Jam*, especially P. J. Williams, Joe Lucido, Bob Weatherly, Austin Stickney, Drew Brooks, Adam Pate, Chris Skinner, and all at Egan's Bar. #sportsthursday

To all of the people I've ever ran twos, threes, fours, or fives with: Matt Parolie, Tim Oliu, Adam Shook, Ryan Tigera, Marc Cevasco, Mike Fitzgerald, John Wixted, Joe Darrow, Brian Ballantine, Rob Cramer, Joe Chandler, Lucas Southworth, Ryan Browne, John Wingard, B.J. Hollars, David Welch, Brittany Travers, Austin Whitver, Michael Marberry, Rob Dixon, Matt Mahaney, Chris Mink, and all the others who knew to watch for the left-hand scoop.

To Tasha: all the Xs and Os.

To my family: especially Mom, Dad, Oma, Nan, and Gramps— as well as those I carry with me: Avi and Ian. I pick you all first.

And, finally, to you, reader. *Boomshakalaka.*

MORE COBALT PRESS TITLES

Four Fathers: short fiction and poetry ($15.00)
Dave Housley, BL Pawelek, Ben Tanzer
and Tom Williams

Black Krim: A Novel ($15.00)
Kate Wyer

Cobalt Review, Volume 3: 2014 ($12.00)
Interviews with Nick Hornby and Mary Miller, 2014 prize
winners and finalists, and more

Thumbnail 6: Flash Fiction ($10.00)
Guest edited by Aubrey Hirsch, featuring works by Matt Bell,
Amber Sparks, xTx, Douglas Cole, Amy Weldon, and more...

How We Bury Our Dead: poetry ($14.00)
Jonathan Travelstead

A Horse Made of Fire: poetry
Heather Bell
Due August 2015

To submit unsolicited manuscripts, or to receive more information
about Cobalt Press publications, including our quarterly and
annual literary journals, visit **www.cobaltreview.com**.